MW01482653

404
00

Rainer Mund/Günther Münch

STRAIGHT GOLF

THE BASICS OF GOOD GOLF

Meyer & Meyer Sport

Original title: „Tele-Golf Band 1 und 2"
© 1996 by Meyer & Meyer Verlag, Aachen
Translated by James Beachus

Die Deutsche Bibliothek – CIP Einheitsaufnahme

Münch, Günther:
Straight golf : The basics of good golf / Günther Münch/Rainer Mund.
[Transl. by James Beachus]. – Aachen : Meyer und Meyer, 1998
Dt. Ausg. u.d.T.: Mund, Rainer: Tele-Golf
ISBN 3-89124-503-3

© 1998 by Meyer & Meyer Verlag, Aachen (Germany)
Olten (CH), Wien (A), Oxford (GB), Québec (CDN),
Lansing/Michigan (USA), Findon/Adelaide (AUS),
Auckland (NZ), Sandton/Johannisburg (ZA)
Cover Photo: Harry Steinheuser, Köln
Diagrams: Florian Pfeffer, Bremen
Cover and Type design: Walter J. Neumann N&N Design-Studio, Aachen
Cover exposure: frw, Reiner Wahlen, Aachen
Exposure: frw, Reiner Wahlen, Aachen
Editorial: Dr. Irmgard Jaeger, Aachen
Typesetting: Novarese
Print: Burg Verlag & Druck, Gastinger GmbH und Co. KG, Stolberg
ISBN 3-89124-503-3
Printed in Germany

CONTENTS

CONTENTS

Part One

Foreword

It took seven years to complete our production of the Golf-Method TV series for the German TV programme WDR. Originally this book was intended to supplement that TV programme series, and give the golfing fraternity yet more information. However the book also serves to banish the many myths and untruths about the sport of golf, which on the one hand are so enormously fascinating, but which on the other hand tend to distract from the facts. This book deals with the facts - straight golf!

All the explanations in the book are valid for the 'right-handed' player. For 'left-handed' players, or for those who swing back onto their left shoulder, then one must reverse the thought process.

In order to avoid the inconvenience of having to refer to a glossary at the end of the book, we decided to give the meaning of special golf terms immediately after they have been mentioned in the text. So whenever the term reappears, the meaning has already been given, and it follows that in this way one automatically becomes more the golfer, with a deeper understanding of the exciting world of this sport.

Rainer Mund
Günther Münch

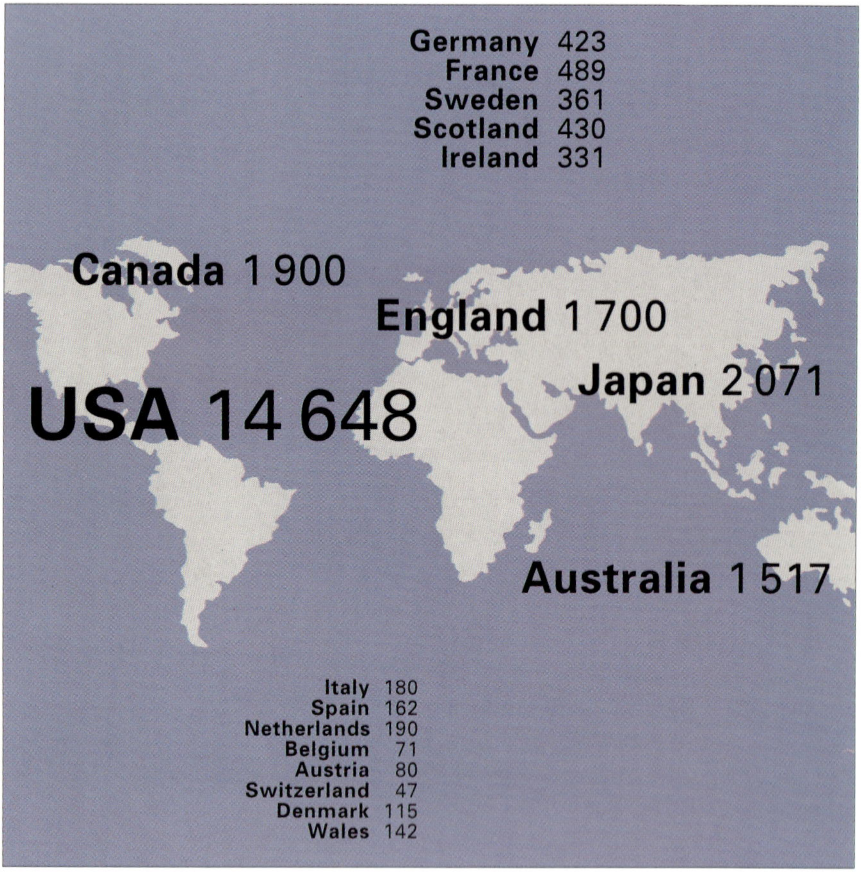

Germany 423
France 489
Sweden 361
Scotland 430
Ireland 331

Canada 1 900

England 1 700

Japan 2 071

USA 14 648

Australia 1 517

Italy 180
Spain 162
Netherlands 190
Belgium 71
Austria 80
Switzerland 47
Denmark 115
Wales 142

Golfplätze auf der Welt

Diagram 1:
The great golf nations

The Fascination of Golf

Irrespective of how good he is, when the golfer hits the ball, a vibrating sensation fills his whole body. He really 'feels' the stroke. There is hardly a feedback in sport that is as fascinating and gripping as this feeling when a good stroke is made. Most golfers, at this point, give vent to their emotions and 'celebrate' their successful stroke. In the same moment the real motivation of the golf player comes into being - the impatience of waiting for the next good stroke.

Golf is a world sport. Wherever you go on holiday there will be a golf-course nearby. Even in the remotest corners of the world, golf is played - be it China, the erstwhile Soviet Union, Kenya or the Philippines. Most of the golf-courses are in the English speaking countries (Diagram 1).

Whenever the Dutch and the British sometimes argue about who was the first person to swing the golf-club, it actually was the British Colonials who brought this sport into the world. At that time the first courses were called 'Golf Links' or 'Links Courses'. They were to be found close to coastal areas in marshy countryside, where the numerous hillocks almost naturally created the playing areas. One only needed to mark the tee-off points and place a flag into a hole at a suitable distance and there you had a golf-course.

Most of the courses today appear somewhat different because they lie more inland. One comes across more natural vegetation, deep rough grass (called the 'rough') and there is always a prevailing wind. There are more trees and numerous water and sand obstacles on a continental championship golf-course. Such a 'modern' golf-course is laid out with tee-off points for Ladies, Men and Professionals (Diagram 2). In this way, the differing playing strengths are balanced out. To the right and left of the playing area (called 'Fairway') there is the 'rough' (long grass). You will find 'bunkers' (a sand filled obstacle or hazard) or water obstacles designed to

11

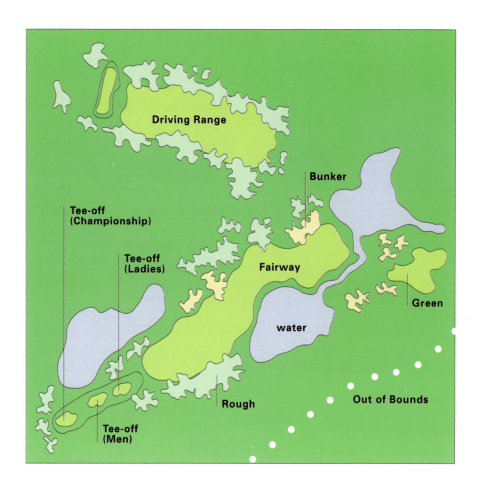

Diagram 2:
The parts of a typical golf-course

'trap' the ball. Also the 'green' (area around the target hole) is surrounded by bunkers. This means you will have to strike the ball so that it lands outside these hazards. Today's golf-courses are equipped with large training areas (called 'driving ranges'). This is where training takes place and where the player can play his eye in and warm-up before a 'round' (a complete game) of golf.

13

The Handicap System

The handicap system allows players of varying strength to be able to play against each other. Good players have a lower handicap figure while the beginner is given either no figure or has a high 'handicap' figure (up to '36'). This figure of 36 varies between countries - e.g. in Germany the handicap for men is 36 while in UK it is 28. In UK the handicap figure of 36 is valid for women and boys.

After a 'round' of golf, the handicap figure is subtracted from the number of strokes each player has made, i.e. the better player has less subtracted than the weaker player.

This is the way that each result played leads towards the status of golf professional ('pro') - that is a person who plays in competitions in contrast to the term 'club professional' who is a golf coach or trainer. The pro has a handicap of '0' - the term used for this handicap standard is "a 'scratch' golfer". Each golf-course has a laid down number for the 'standard' - this is normally 72 strokes. This represents the maximum number of strokes that the player with handicap '0' is expected to take.

A beginner with a handicap of 36 would expect to take 108 strokes for the course.

In most countries the official handicap begins with the figure '36' (beginner). To reach this standard takes quite a while. Nevertheless club pro's (golf trainers in clubs) allow players to play despite not having a handicap.

Let us take an example: If the course has a standard of 72 then the handicap 10 player should get round in 82 strokes. If he takes 85 strokes then he is 3 strokes over his handicap. If a handicap 0 player takes 76 strokes then he is 4 strokes over his handicap and would have lost against the handicap 10 player.

Besides the net results (as above with the handicap system), naturally there is also a competitive basis of actual strokes taken - i.e. the least strokes taken is the winner. Proper championship rounds and all the professional tournaments are scored on this basis.

There is no rule on how long it will take for one to gain a handicap. For some golfers it takes years before they can reach a handicap of 36. Others get there almost straight away. Again others find difficulty at the beginning and then suddenly come forward in a rush.

Whether one will get down to a single figure is largely dependent on the quality of the basic training, how hard one practices and the natural talent. The more intensity one places in the first stages of training and the more one understands, the greater the chance of being able to realize and exploit one's personal ability.

PAR

There are three different types of 'holes' (a golf-course consists of 18 holes). According to the number of 'shots' (strokes) that a golf professional will need to take on a hole, one speaks of PAR-3, PAR-4 and PAR-5 holes. It is assumed that within the figure there will be a requirement to use 2 putts (strokes to roll the ball into the hole). Accordingly the greens categorised as PAR-3 can be reached with the first shot. For a PAR-4 green a professional can normally reach the green in two shots. Put another way round, a player is said to reach the green (putting area) in 'regulation' figures, if for example on a PAR-3 he is on the putting area in one stroke, and to a PAR-4 in two strokes. The length of the fairway for a PAR-5 hole is calculated so that a professional will take two or three shots to reach the green.

If it requires three shots to hole out on a PAR-3 hole then this is called PAR. When the number of shots for all 18 holes are added together, using the PAR ratings - normally around 70 (see above) - then this signifies the standard for the particular golf-course.

15

COMPETITION				DATE		Handicap	Strokes Received

PLAYER A

PLAYER B

Front nine:

Marker's Score	No.	Black Yards	Par	Stroke Index	Score A	Score B	W=+ I=− H=0
	1	348	4	11			
	2	311	4	7			
	3	320	4	13			
	4	514	5	5			
	5	141	3	17			
	6	399	4	3			
	7	324	4	9			
	8	326	4	15			
	9	244	3	1			
	OUT	2927	35				

Back nine:

Marker's Score	No.	Black Yards	Par	Stroke Index	Score A	Score B	W=+ I=− H=0
	10	191	3	14			
	11	348	4	10			
	12	311	4	6			
	13	320	4	12			
	14	514	5	4			
	15	141	3	18			
	16	399	4	2			
	17	324	4	8			
	18	326	4	16			
	IN	2874	35				
	OUT	2927	35				
	TOTAL	5801	70				

HANDICAP

NETT

MARKER'S SIGNATURE

PLAYER'S SIGNATURE

RESULT

PAR 70   S.S.S. 70

Diagram 3: A typical score card

16

Generally speaking the PAR rating is determined by the length of the fairway:
PAR-3 - up to 250 yards
PAR-4 - 220 - 500 yards
PAR-5 - over 440 yards

There are, however, golf-courses where there will be deviations from the rule of length. For example where a fairway lies on a downward slope, with the hole 450 yards from the tee-off, it could still be counted as a PAR-4.

Each golf-course has its own score card on which the length and PAR rating of each hole is given (see - "a typical score card" in Diagram 3). You will see a column labelled 'Stroke Index' and this gives the order of difficulty of each of the holes. In Diagram 3 the score card shows that the most difficult hole is number 9 (stroke index 1) and the easiest is number 15 (stroke index 18). After each hole you enter the number of shots taken by your opponent onto the score card. At the end of a competition the score card is signed by the player and the person who has counted the number of shots taken (marker's signature).

Internationally, the language of golf is invariably the English language. Perhaps the most popular expression used by golfers is the word 'birdie'. The term birdie means that one has taken one shot less than PAR to hole out. If it takes six shots to hole out on a PAR-5 hole then the term 'bogey' is used. If you achieve a 'double-bogey' (two strokes over PAR) on all 18 holes, you would end up with a handicap of 36 - try working out the sum! The following list gives the expressions which are used world-wide:

Albatross	three strokes under PAR
Eagle	two strokes under PAR
Birdie	one stroke under PAR
Par	As PAR
Bogey	one stroke over PAR
Double-bogey	two strokes over PAR
Triple-bogey	three strokes over PAR

Don't be surprised if initially you find that for the first few sessions on the golf-course there is no expression for the number of strokes that you play. Even the authors of this book took sometimes 8,9 or 10 strokes for each hole, in the first few weeks of playing golf.

17

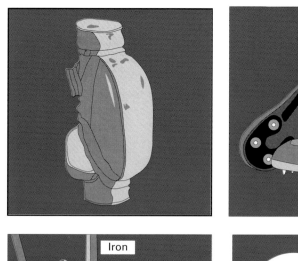
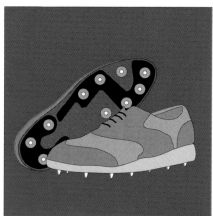
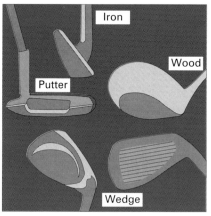

Diagram 4:
Golfing equipment

18

Equipment

Equipment plays an especially large role in golf. Until you have a suitable set of equipment you will not be able to exploit your potential to the full. This doesn't mean lots of flashy coloured golf-clubs and an expensive golf bag. It means the RIGHT golf-club for you, some good shoes, a few golf balls, golf T's (small wooden or plastic pegs to rest the ball on for the tee-off) and a small golf bag (see Diagram 4). We DON'T consider the famous golfing glove a necessity at the beginning.

SHOES

At the beginning low profiled (flat soled) jogging shoes are perfectly adequate for training. Becoming increasingly more popular are such shoes fitted with screw-in spikes made of artificial material. As soon as you are able to achieve a certain regularity in your golf activities - and also before you go to the expense of buying a complete set of clubs (see below) - you will need some proper golfing shoes (with spikes screwed into the sole). You will be spending a long time wearing these shoes and also will put quite a few miles behind you in them. Therefore be advised to buy some really good ones. Shoes which have been found to be particularly suitable are those with ceramic tipped spikes as these do not wear out too easily.

GOLF BALLS

Practically any golf ball is a good ball. You are well advised to stick with one particular make as you will get used to its feel and sound. Look for the data regarding 'pitch'.

GOLF BAGS

Even the smallest golf bag will have room enough for a complete set of golf-clubs as well as the requisite number of balls and golf T's. Besides

19

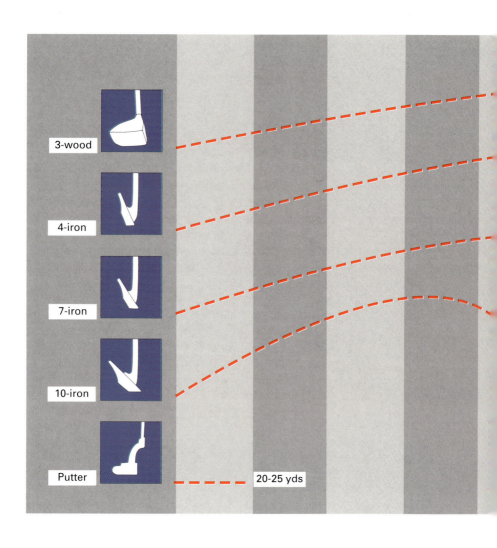

Diagram 5: The various ball trajectories

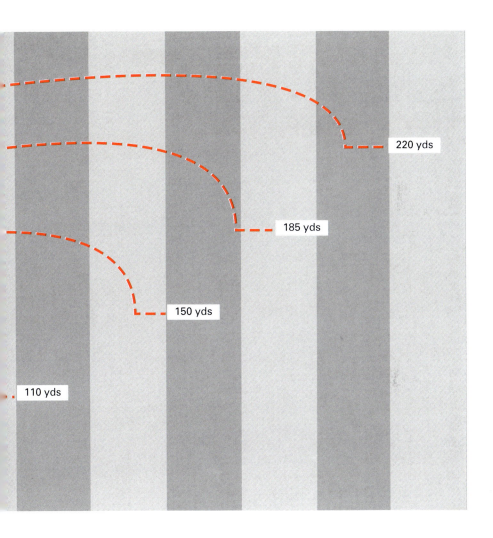

220 yds

185 yds

150 yds

110 yds

this it lends itself to the sporting prowess of the game of golf. If you are relatively fit, don't be afraid to carry your complete golf equipment in a SMALL golf bag on your shoulder. Don't worry about your shoulders - carrying the bag is much healthier than the other popular version of pulling a so-called golf trolley (small barrow-like apparatus with no engine on which the golf bag fits). This causes your spine to rotate with the pressure of pulling. We would also recommend that you change the carrying shoulder at each hole. This sounds perhaps unusual but it does you good. As a reader of this book you belong to the fraternity of golfers who want to learn new golf habits - why not do something which benefits your health at the same time.

Only when it is raining does the golf trolley come into its own, as it allows you to concentrate on the grip of the golf-club - you are freer to move about. Should you take a golfing holiday in the USA sometime, you will come across the third variation of this theme - the electric golf car. It is clear that this detracts from the sporting value somewhat. They are useful however for people with a physical handicap - without the electric golf car they would not be able to play golf.

GOLF-CLUBS

Regarding golf-clubs one makes the distinction between 'woods' and 'irons'. There are two main principles: the longer the club the lower the ANGLE of the FACE (LOFT) on the part of the club which strikes the ball - and, the lower the ANGLE of attack the farther and the flatter (in flight) the ball will travel (see Diagram 5).

Woods

The so-called woods have not been made out of wood for a long time. More often they are made out of hightech materials and are used for the long distance strokes (over 200 yds). This is why they have longer shafts and larger volume club-heads.

22

Irons

Irons are used for the immediate approach shots to the flag as they allow far more precision of the stroke than the woods. You could also use an iron for a stroke at a distance of 150 yds or more as an approach shot. One differentiates between the irons as 'long' irons (1-4), 'medium' irons (5-7) and 'short' irons (8-10).

Wedges

The Pitching Wedge (PW) (or 10-iron) is used for the short strokes (especially under 100 yds) which must come to standstill rapidly.

The Sandwedge (SW) (or sand-iron) is used for all shots taken in sand near the flag, and it can be used for particularly short, high trajectory approach shots, for example to overcome an obstacle.

Putter

The putter has hardly any angle (loft) on the face of the clubhead. On a club without any angle the striking face is vertical to the ground. The more the angle on the striking face, the more the face points into the sky. The putter is used to carry out the 'putt' - the stroke to roll the ball on the green - the smooth short grass surrounding the hole. The putter can also be used for strokes just outside the green.

Chipper

Of all the various special clubs, we believe one worth mention is the 'chipper' (a sort of putter with a loft angle). Later on, it will prove to be very useful (see Diagram 6).

In order to become familiar with the golf swing one can best get into the rhythm for a few weeks using a MEDIUM IRON (5,6,7) and a PUTTER.

Once one begins to strike the ball with regularity, then it is worth PURCHASING A 'HALF SET' OF CLUBS. A HALF set consists of those irons with uneven numbers, a 3-wood and a putter. This has the advantage of you learning your way round the golf bag, as well as learning the connection between ball trajectory and the choice of club. A 3-wood for long shots is perfectly adequate at this stage.

23

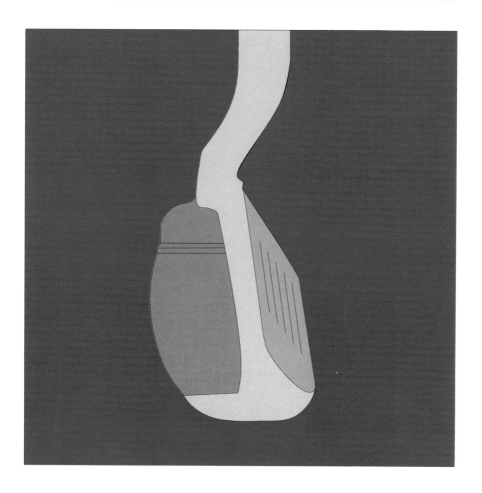

Diagram 6:
The chipper

24

> **TIP** If you can find a golf partner, we recommend that you buy a set of golf-clubs together and divide them between yourselves. One buys the even numbered clubs (4,6,8,PW) and the other the uneven numbered clubs (3,5,7,9,SW).

Don't be put off or confused by the large variety of shaft and golf clubs on offer. Only purchase a whole set of golf-clubs when you can hit the ball regularly. Only then will you be in a position to be able to 'feel' the differences.

Insist on TRYING OUT DIFFERENT SHAFTS (more important than the clubhead). Take advice from a professional and make sure THAT THE GOLF CLUB MATCHES YOUR ANATOMY (SIZE, STRENGTH).

> **TIP** You will have the correct shaft when you can really perceive the weight of the golf clubhead when you make a chip shot (see below) as well as when you take a full shot. You can note this first at the end of a day playing lots of golf rather than in the first ten minutes on the golf-course. All too many amateurs use shafts which are too stiff. Just remember that many Tour Pros (Professionals) use a flexible so-called 'regular' shaft simply because they can 'feel' the clubhead better.

You must realise, that the amount of flexibility there is in the shaft is dependent on the speed of your stroke. Only when the shaft can bend enough, will you be in a position to be able to 'feel' the golf clubhead.

25

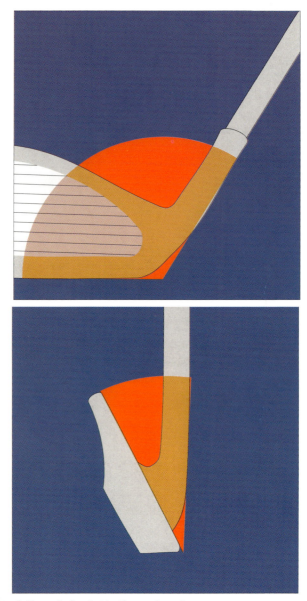

Diagram 7: Loft (from below), Lie (from above)

TIP You can check whether a golf-club is 'right' for you by noting the following:

Once you have taken-up your position as if you were going to strike the ball, (see "Address" and "Direction"), someone standing opposite you should be able to push a sheet of normal paper under half of the clubhead. The angle at which the shaft is moulded into the clubhead forms the so-called 'lie' against your height (see Diagram 7). Do not confuse the 'lie' with the 'loft', which is the angle of the face of the clubhead, and determines the trajectory of the ball (height and distance). You can easily imagine that a more upright lie is more suitable for the taller player, and, a flatter lie better for the smaller person. The more the lie suits you, the more natural will be your stance when addressing the ball.

27

Golf Gymnastics

Before you really get down to it, you must understand a few medical truths about sport.

The golf swing is a ONE-SIDED (elliptical) movement. On the other hand there are cyclic movements (e.g. jogging) in which one uses similar muscles on both sides of the body, and which do not lead to a loss of balance. When you play golf regularly certain muscles on one side of the body become particularly developed. There will also be a shortening of certain muscles. Thus there will be some strain and an imbalance of the muscular structure in the whole body.

It is not sufficient to have a regular massage. In order to avoid aches and pains which result from this one-sided movement, you will have to be active. If you play a lot of golf and do not take gymnastic exercises to recuperate, you will endanger your health.

Wrong or over-stretched movements at the beginning of a day of golf can lead to bad injuries. Before a round of golf we seriously recommend that you go through a short warming-up programme of exercises, and, additionally you should take regular recuperative gymnastic exercises which you can carry out separately from golf - not only after a round but also at home or combined with a run in the woods.

Pure golf related gymnastics, which have been developed by us, will be found in „Straight Golf - Part 2". However, the most important points are as follows:-

Firstly, ensure that you have a good blood circulation (e.g. running on the spot, crouch jumps). Stretch your legs, arms, shoulder blades and rear and hips. AVOID WHIPPING MOVEMENTS.

One popular method is particularly unsuitable, and this is the practice of placing the golf-club over the shoulders with the arms wrapped over the ends, and carrying out fast half-rotations of the upper body. Instead, using this method, twist yourself until you feel a slight strain and then hold the position for 20-30 seconds. You can also do this by standing with your back against a wall and turning your chest until you can lay your hand flat on the wall. Stretch the muscles on the rear and sides of your legs. To do this, sit cross-legged and pull your knees back. Do stretching exercises to the side.

If you are one of those people who has taken up golf for pure health reasons, we recommend that in addition to the warming-up exercises above, strengthening exercises should also be carried out. Take the trouble to discuss all this with a physiotherapist. We do not recommend training on exercise machines unless you have been carrying out power training for some time or have been under a professional eye. As a recuperative sport to golf we recommend backstroke swimming.

The Grip

The grip of your hands is the contact with the golf-club. The feeling comes from here. It also determines the arc of the swing. There are some other more important points:

The enormous power which is created by the golf swing can only be transferred to the ball by using the correct grip.

If your hands are holding the club in a clumsy fashion, your body will seek to correct this. This results in a pulled swing. If you get accustomed to an incorrect grip you will spend the rest of your "golfing career" trying to correct this at the expense of a lot of strain on the body.

Because of this we will take some time in this section to get it right - do the same with your grip!

Training Exercise

a) Stand upright. Let both your arms hang loosely on each side of your body. Ask a friend to place a club (e.g. a 7-iron) into the fingers of your left hand. Ensure that the end of the grip protrudes about 1/4 - 1/2 inch out of the palm of the hand i.e. the end is not lying in the palm.

b) You will find that you now make a natural movement in the direction of the club as you actively tighten your grip. Now try to do this again but AVOID the natural tendency to move forward. Take hold of the club grip. Just wrap your fingers round the grip with the thumb resting in the palm of the hand and pointing down the shaft. That's all you have to do - you cannot grip any better with the left hand anyway (see Diagram 8).

c) Repeat this several times. You will notice that the club is gripped by the fingers and not the main part of the hand. This is important because you have considerably more tactile feeling in the fingers (particularly in the ends of your fingers) than in the hand itself. Fingers play an important and dominant role in the movement of the hands when carrying out a swing. Even if you have weak hands you will be able to lift the golf club up to a level with your eyes.

d) Now put the little finger of the right hand into the crevice formed by the forefinger and middle finger of your left hand (see Diagram 9). If you believe you have particularly weak finger muscles, or your hands are very small, you can intertwine the fingers as they meet each other (see Diagram 'Interlocking'). You intertwine the FOREFINGER of the left hand trapping the LITTLE FINGER of the right hand. Whether you adopt this way of gripping is up to you. If you can feel the bones of the fingers with your finger tips then you have them correctly intertwined.

It is important that the next finger (the ring finger) of the right hand lies fully next to the other finger of the left hand on the grip. The same applies to your middle and forefingers (see Diagram 10).

e) As a last point make sure that the left thumb tucks up into the hollow of the right palm. This hollow is made for the golfer so that you can tuck the thumb into the spot nice and comfortably. The PALMS of your HANDS will now lie diametrically OPPOSITE each other.

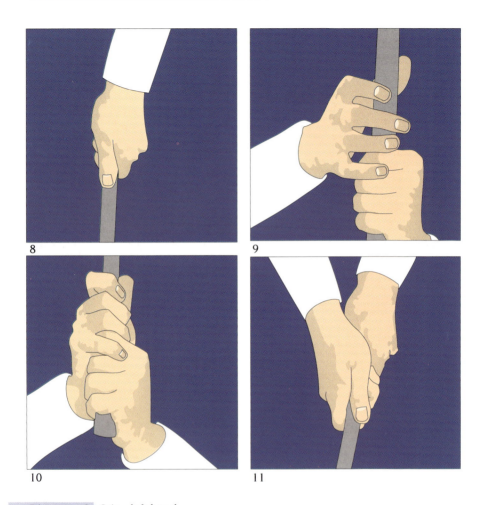

Diagram 8: Grip - left hand
Diagram 9: This is how you lay the right hand over the left
Diagram 10: "Overlapping" - view from underneath
Diagram 11: "Overlapping" - view from above

Diagram 12:
Alternative to the overlapping grip: "Interlocking"

33

If your right thumb is not automatically lying against the grip, twist it round to the left. The thumb must not apply pressure on the club from above. The gap between the right forefinger and the thumb should form a 'V' when you look down at your hands - for someone standing opposite this will be an upside down 'V' (see Diagram 11).

Your grip on the club is now optimized, but is only perfect when you can place the clubhead on the ground so that all of the 'sole' (bottom) area of the club lies on the ground, and that the face of the club is pointing in the direction of the target. The 'V' form in the left hand should now point approximately at your right shoulder. Lay your right hand over the left thumb and look where the 'V' on this hand is pointing - it should also point to the right shoulder.

You can only make a clumsy mistake now if you turn your right hand too far to the right. If you do this the 'V' will point too far to the right shoulder. If the palm of your right hand creeps too far under the club grip it will not be diametrically opposite the palm of the left hand. Correct this mistake and create a 'NEUTRAL' grip so that the palms are opposite each other.

Without doubt, to find the right grip at the beginning, it seems that the more care you take to get it right, the more unusual it feels. But it does mean later on you will have more fun playing. If you can assimilate all this information into a 'feel' for the grip you will hardly give this point a second thought. You will be sure every time that you have adopted the same right grip. Up until this point you should CONSTANTLY CHECK your grip regularly.

You have got the right grip if :
... you can see 2-3 knuckles of the left hand (see Diagram 11)
... you can see a 'V' between the thumb and the forefinger of both hands (see Diagrams 8 & 11)
... the 'V's' point approximately to the right shoulder
... the end of the grip is protruding a little out of the left hand (see Diagram 10)

34

TIP To accelerate the learning process, obtain just the grip part of the shaft, which you can pick up and grip whether you are at home, in the office or indeed anywhere. In this way you will be able to exercise a light grip - the grip part of the shaft is hollow as you will recognize. Just imagine it is filled with toothpaste and you don't really want to squeeze it out!

The Address Position

The correct address position begins where the grip ends. If your grip is wrong even the best of stances won't help you. If your grip is correct then you need the right way to position yourself. Only when these two are correct will you have the possibility of developing your talent.

To talk about certain angles the body must form, is in our opinion, of little help. You have to 'feel' the correct address and above all, always be able to adopt it.

The following method has proved itself:

Training Exercise a) Ask a friend to blindfold you, and then, with his arms stretched out, to gently push you until you begin to lose your balance. Before you do fully lose balance, bend your upper body slightly forwards and bend your knees a little so as not to fall over. You can also grasp your hands together or lift them up to the same effect. Concentrate on managing to hold your address position. Remember you don't know which side your friend is coming from.

35

Diagram 13:
The body angles and the position of the shoulders over the knees

36

b) Now get your friend to push you from all four sides until you begin to lose your balance. Each time renew your address position.

c) Carry out this exercise several times - each time bending your knees more until they form a right angle. This is quite strenuous, but it will teach you the correct feeling for the body angle.

d) Repeat the exercise for a last time. Now bend your knees not quite so much and stand with your upper body leaning slightly forward. Take off the blindfold. Shake your muscles, which have probably tightened up, and let your arms hang loosely by your sides.

Check whether:
... You are standing with your legs apart i.e. your feet are firmly placed.
... You are holding your weight on the soles of your feet i.e. well balanced.
... You can feel your body tension (an important point) right from your feet to your head.
... Your backbone is straight - from your head to your bottom.

These points are the standard elements of a good address position. Only when you can master these points will you be able to make fine adjustments. A good position is shown in Diagram 13.

Pick up your club and set the sole of the clubhead flat on the ground. Stand with slightly bent knees as UPRIGHT AS POSSIBLE. Don't push your behind to the rear over-exaggeratedly. Lift your chin off your chest so that YOUR HEAD AND YOUR REAR form A STRAIGHT LINE with the spine. Your CENTRE OF GRAVITY now lies over the MIDDLE OF YOUR FEET.

37

Diagram 14:
The shoulders fit between the feet.

This will be the case when your armpits are centred in a line over your kneecaps and the centre of your feet arches.

Watch your balance. You can do this by ensuring your feet are spread apart sufficiently. Stand so that YOUR SHOULDERS WOULD FIT BETWEEN YOUR FEET (see Diagram 14).

Each time that you think that you are not sure if you are standing in the 'middle', briefly shut your eyes and imagine that someone wants to push you off balance. Practice your address until you find you automatically pick it up correctly.

If you have taken the time to train your body into the correct position, you will have avoided what the majority of amateur golfers find as an hindrance in ADVANCING their game - this is the unsuitability of the address for taking the swing.

TIP To check your address, we recommend that you have a video taken of yourself holding varying lengths of clubs. You will quickly recognize whether you are standing relaxed and in a natural position when addressing the ball, and you will be able to improve your address in this way.

Direction and Aiming

As a matter of principle the connecting line between the toes of your feet, your hips and your shoulders should all point in the same direction. You can check this by laying a club in line with your toes, and taking another club, hold this in turn by the hips and the shoulders. The feet should be parallel to the line of the aim. Your knees, hips and shoulders should also be parallel with the line to the target (see Diagram 15). THE DIRECTION OF THE FRONT FACE OF THE CLUB IS PARTICULARLY RELEVANT TO THE AIM (see Diagram 16).

Diagram 15:
Aiming for a straight shot

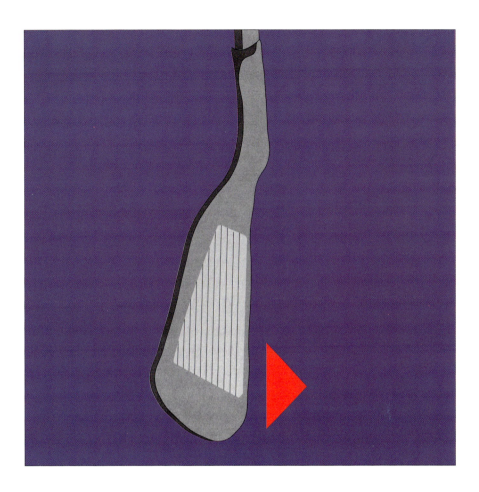

Diagram 16:
The CLUBFACE points in the direction of the target.

The Philosophy of the Swing

Terminology in the sport of golf uses the word 'swing'. One 'swings' the golf-club, or, one has the 'right swing' - and so on and so forth. It follows then that because of the use of this word, it has particular characteristics. Although the contemporary expression and word 'golf stroke' are more often used in professional golf, it does help those, who have yet to master this, to imagine it still as a swing.

The key to successful golf largely lies in the synchronisation of arm and body movement. When you think of a golf SWING then the arms and hands are brought dominantly into play. This will be the case for all those who have not played golf for years.

You must imagine that the upper body represents the 'swing' motor and the clubhead as the object to be swung. The arms and the shaft can then be considered as the 'transmission chain'.

THE SWING

In order to realize the weight of the golf-club, take an iron in your hand and lay one end in the palm of your left hand and the other end in your right. Now guess the weight in each of your hands - in ounces or grams.

In the one hand you will feel hardly any weight, but in the other there will be some weight felt. Whichever is the heavier of the two, is where the clubhead lies. We will leave it to you and your club pro to weigh it on the scales in order to check your estimate. The swing moment - an expression you will hear spoken of amongst the better players - is nothing more than the relation of the weight of the two ends of the club to each other. The heavier the clubhead is in relation to the grip end, the higher the swing moment.

42

Changes in the swing moment are more easily perceived actually during the swing than with the club at rest because of the forces created in the swing movement.

YOUR FORM ON THE DAY

On some days it will seem that the weight of the clubhead is heavier than other days. Each day we perceive things differently and we seem to have different capabilities also. This is particularly noticeable when you might have drunk alcohol the night before and you are playing golf with a thick head. In this case your capabilities will certainly be impaired - accordingly you will have a bad day. Just as alcohol will have an effect, there are other factors which will have some influence on your performance in this complex and challenging game.

It is impossible to define all the factors which will affect your game - there are so many of them. Sleepless nights and little personal psychological disturbances are probably the most important factors which will affect you in the pattern of living a healthy life.

It will be important for you to realize that you must work up to your best form each time you are about to play a round of golf. It is exactly this action which decides the strength of a top player, and there is no reason why you, like the pros, should not learn what you have to do to get into top form. In practice it looks like this:

> **TIP** Take the trouble at the beginning of a day of golf to get the feel of each of your golf-clubs and their 'true' weight. If you are having a bad day they will feel too light. Relax and practice your swing until you can actually feel the exact number of ounces in the clubhead.

On days when you feel particularly unsure of yourself we recommend the following training exercise for the swing:

Training Exercise

a) Put your right hand behind your back, and take a medium iron (e.g. a 6-iron) in your other hand and hold it with only the forefinger and middle finger in a pincer-grip (like a pair of pliers) from the grip end. Stand with your feet apart (shoulder-width) and now try to get the club, which is hanging down, to swing like a pendulum by moving the weight of your BODY from one leg onto the other.

b) Take some time on this. Concentrate your mind on the inner feelings of the body. You will now begin to realize that the club is swinging because you will not only feel the weight of the club in your fingers, but also in your body. The motion of the club is transmitted from the motion of your body, similar to the motion of a child on a SWING as it moves backwards and forwards.

Carry out this exercise until you do feel the weight of the club in unison with your body. If you find it difficult just shut your eyes. After a while you will experience the feeling.

The Swing Technique

The technique of the golf swing is, without doubt, very complex. In our opinion there are very few important points which can be referred to regarding how one can understand and learn the swing. Most of the points spring out automatically from the solid basic principles of the grip, stance and posture.

In actual fact there are only two MAIN MOTIONS: the ROTATION of the upper body AND the way the BALANCE CHANGES during this movement. If you stand with your feet shoulder-width apart (and, of course, bending slightly forward), and you turn your shoulders to the right so that your back is pointing to the target, your balance will regulate itself automatically.

If you consider where your centre of balance is (looking at it from the player's point of view) this will move first of all to the right and then come back again - in the golf swing however the shoulders also come back and travel through until the chest is pointing at the target.

Take an iron or a wood and adopt a grip position. Put the golf ball just to the left of a middle line opposite your feet - and in the case of a wood yet a little further to the left. A triangle will be formed between the left and right shoulder and the grip (see Diagram 17).

Your arms are connected to your shoulders and follow to a certain degree a constant parabola in the swing movement. In order to do this properly the joints of, the arms and wrists should not be used. Your arms and rib cage will move in unison and the triangular form is maintained (see Diagram 18).

Diagram 17:
Triangle formed between the left and right shoulder and the grip.

46

Diagram 18:
Arms and rib cage move in unison.

Diagram 19:
Your wrists stay at the same distance in front of the chest.
Your rib cage turns against a locked right leg position.

48

Training Exercise

a) Lay your left hand on your right chest and your right hand on your left chest. Your upper arms are now lying parallel to the sides of your body. The contact between the rib cage and your arms makes this an easy movement. Holding this position take-up your address and rotate your shoulders as if you were swinging a golf-club. Your arms still stay close to your body.

b) Now let your arms hang down and take-up a golf-club in your hands in a loose grip. Turn your shoulders again. Despite using a light grip it now seems more difficult because you have your arms and the club to contend with. You can compare it with a pirouette. The nearer your arms are to your body, the easier and faster is the circular movement.

The training exercise above shows you that the clubhead is rotated by the swinging movement of the rib cage. The weight of the club, and using a light grip, will AUTOMATICALLY CAUSE THE WRISTS TO BEND (see Diagram 19). Between the CLUB and the FOREARMS there is now more of an ANGLE. Your hands (grip) stay nevertheless at the SAME DISTANCE IN FRONT of the chest.

The more you are able to coil up your muscles, the less you will be able to rotate your shoulders, and this is correct. The coiling reaction is created by TURNING THE RIB CAGE WHILE KEEPING YOUR RIGHT LEG LOCKED IN POSITION.

In this way your centre of balance moves more and more onto the right leg and 'behind' the ball (see Diagram 20). You can improve and increase the tension (like a coiled spring) by pointing your right foot more towards the target. When your right leg adopts the same position each time, the muscular tension created will be more constant.

49

Interestingly enough it is exactly this position of the right leg which is successfully demonstrated by world class players, who have an identical position when addressing the ball, as well as at the top of their backswing. Watch out for the right leg position of Nick Faldo, Jose Maria Olazabal or Bernhard Langer.

At the highest point of the backswing the club points in a direction parallel to the flag (see Diagram 21). This is an important point so that the energy in the club at the moment of impact with the ball sends it in the direction of the target. Good players can make deductions regarding the technique by observing the position of the club at the highest point of the backswing. If the club slants away to the left of the line to the target, the energy force will tend to also move in that direction. It will then depend on the position of the clubface as to where the ball will go in the end.

The chain reaction which follows is made up of several flowing impulses, which result from the turn of the body and the change in the centre of balance in a neutral address position. In due course the flow of your swing will be more successful.

The clubhead now drags behind the turning movement of the body. UPPER BODY AND ARMS FOLLOW THE HIP MOVEMENT (see Diagram 22). If you are particularly talented, the correct angle formed between the forearms and the club will stay consistent after a while. Professionals hold the left arm almost always parallel to the ground when the club is pointing vertically upwards. This is due to the inherent inertia, because your body, especially the hips, is turning across the direction of ball to target.

Concentrate on using YOUR BODY WEIGHT AS THE 'MOTOR' TO ACCELERATE the golf-club. By doing this the weight will be gradually transferred from the right leg onto the left. You move your body by changing the centre of balance in the first instance and in the second by the turn itself (rotation). The enormous power in a golf swing is created in this way and not simply by putting power into hitting the ball. At the moment of impact with the golf ball your arms form almost A STRAIGHT LINE WITH THE GOLF-CLUB (see Diagram 23).

There will be practically no weight on the right leg at all after hitting the ball. The head turns with the body in the direction of the target (see Diagram 24). In this position you will be able to realize how aesthetic and balanced a good golf swing is. The enormous power is captured in the fully balanced posture of the body. The shaft of the club is still bent and flexed and the stroke is almost completed.

In the final posture the balance is fully maintained. The front of the body is facing towards the target. In contrast to the classic golf swing in the early years, the body is standing upright and is relaxed. In this position one could imagine standing close to a wall with no gap between a line from the shin to the shoulder and the wall (see Diagram 25).

At this juncture give yourself time also to assimilate and learn all the differing aspects. If you adopt the right grip and stand well, your golf-club will gradually be in the right position. Your posture and movements will develop on their own. With time your muscles will adapt and become supple and your movements will be more economical.

Diagram 20:
The centre of balance is 'BEHIND' the ball.

52

Diagram 21:
On the backswing the club points in a direction parallel to the flag.

Diagram 22:
The club follows the turn of the body according to the law of inertia.
There is therefore an angle formed between the forearm and the club.

Diagram 23:

In order to transmit the energy of the body movements to an optimum, the arms form a straight line with the golf-club.

55

Diagram 24:
After the moment of impact the whole of the weight is on the left leg.

Diagram 25:
The end of the stroke is relaxed and the posture is UPRIGHT.

57

TIP Pick out ONE of the following 'thoughts' about the swing and practice it until you get the feeling of what it is about. Then go onto another. NB: Dependent on their capabilities, successful golfers tend to be conscientious people and employ the principle of taking things in steps and with care.

Get to know the weight of the clubhead during the swing.

The pressure used in the grip is consistent and the hands never change position.

The backswing movement is clearly shorter than the follow through.

The head remains still.

The right knee stays in the same position during the backswing.

At the end of the backswing the body's centre of balance is behind the ball (c.f. Diagram 20).

The right side of the body (right shoulder, right hip, right ankle) turns with the stroke.

The distance between the hands (grip) and the chest remains constant well after striking the ball.

The eyes leave the ball in unison with the turn of the body.

At the finish of the stroke the whole body is facing the flag.

At the end of the stroke the whole body weight is on the left leg.

At the end of the stroke the balance is fully maintained.

Pre-Shot Routines

You should now understand all about the correct way to carry out the swing. You have also practised the position of your hands (grip), your feet and your body (stance, posture and aiming).

Adopt the following routine, which should become standard practice EACH TIME you make a shot in your golf game from now on. Build the routine into your personality and make it one of the traits of your character. A personal routine will help your muscles to remember the important points for every stroke. Remember the points about your 'form' and also think about 'feeling' the weight of the club. It is up to you how you use all the points in combination with each other, but here is a FRAMEWORK to go from:

Training Exercise

a) Step back AT LEAST THREE paces from the ball.

b) Decide which shot you want to play. Lay the golf-club LOOSELY in the RIGHT hand with its full weight resting on the ground.

c) When you move up to the ball, switch your eyes backwards and forwards from the ball to the target. The club is still sitting loosely in the right hand.

d) With your right hand place the club cleanly behind the ball and line it up, with the underside of the face of the club pointing in the direction of the target. Switch your eyes from the face of the club to the target. Take up your address and place your feet correctly. The club is still sitting loosely in the fingers of the right hand.

e) Before you pull into the backswing, grip the club with both hands. The grip and the backswing mould themselves into one movement.

At the beginning you will need to exercise a considerable amount of drive and determination to keep up this training, but in the long run it will be an aid to your golfing future. When you have settled down into your own pre-shot routine, stick with it and don't make any changes unless it serves as an improvement. Talk about it with your club pro and CARRY OUT THE ROUTINE BEFORE EVERY STROKE.

The Putt

Anyone who has played miniature-golf will know about the putt.

When you played miniature-golf you probably just grabbed the club and didn't think too much about the grip. Whichever grip you use for the putt is generally not important. Make sure, however, that your grip is comfortable and make sure your address is likewise.

THE GRIP

The grip which takes into account the two points above, and which in our opinion offers additional advantages, is the Bernhard Langer-Grip (see below). Irrespective of whichever grip you do decide on, the principles of putting are all the same.

Place your PUTTER WITH THE BASE ON THE GROUND. Now bend over it so that your LEFT ARM IS IN LINE WITH THE SHAFT. If you lean in yet a little more you will be able to stretch your right hand not only round the grip but also you will be able to grip the forearm of your left hand (see Diagram 26). It will take some time before you get used to the unusual position of the hands but in the end it will be worth it.

ADDRESS

Make sure your eyes are immediately over the ball. A handbag mirror placed on a sheet of paper is a useful way of checking this. By doing this you will guarantee that the path from the ball to the hole (the putting line) is direct and will allow correct aiming.

Diagram 26:
The address using the Bernhard Langer-Grip

TECHNIQUE

Most people use their 'feel' for the ball when putting. This leads generally to the use of the wrists to putt. It is exactly this that the Bernhard Langer-Grip will avoid, because the wrists are normally blocked by the shaft end (see Diagrams 27a & 27b). This grip means that the putter hangs down from the shoulder area and swings like a pendulum i.e. it oscillates. Precisely this makes for successful putting.

When you have settled to "your" own address position, practice the pendulum putting swing.

Training Exercise a) SWING
THE PUTTER EQUAL AMOUNTS TO EACH SIDE - LIKE A PENDULUM.
- Mark the centre line with a golf tee or a coin.
- Lay the ball exactly on a line centred between your feet. Swing the putter to the tip of your left foot and then back to the tip of your right one.

b) SWING (LIKE A PENDULUM) WITH AND WITHOUT THE BALL - EQUALLY TO EACH SIDE.
- Do the swing without the ball and 'feel' the weight of the putter head.
- Do the swing now with the ball to get the feel.
- Lay out a line of balls so that you need to take a pace forward each time you play the ball and also so that, in between, you do the swing without the ball. As you do this keep your putting address position and use the legs only to move to the next ball.

c) Do a short pendulum swing = short putt.
d) Do a long pendulum swing = long putt.

63

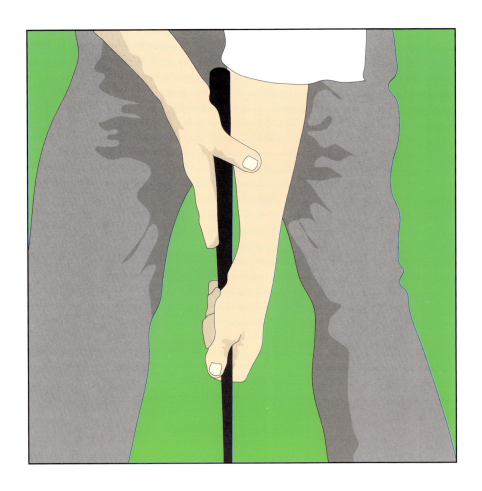

Diagram 27a:
The left wrist is ...

Diagram 27b:
...blocked by the end of the shaft grip.

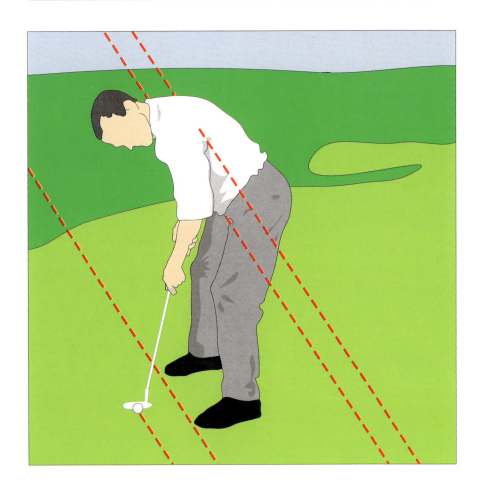

Diagram 28a:
Just as in a normal golf stroke, the line of the feet, hips and shoulders is parallel to ...

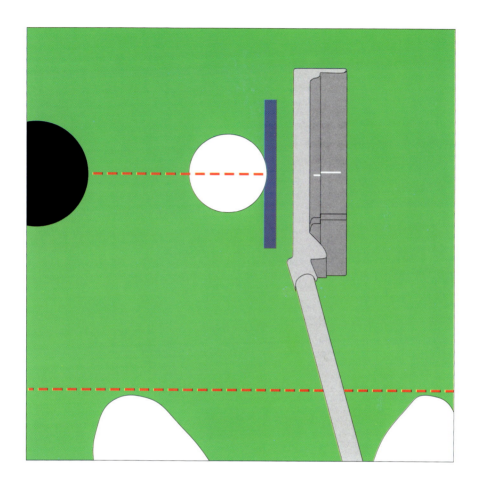

Diagram 28b:
... the line from the face of the putter to the target.

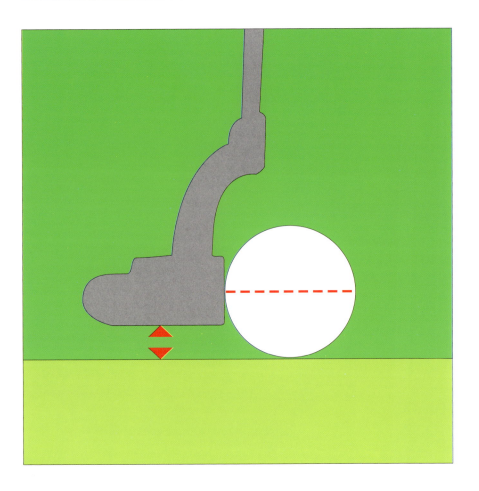

Diagram 29:

In order to align the middle of the face of the putter with the middle of the golf ball, the putter must be raised about half an inch above the ground.

68

It will already be clear to you how similar the principles are becoming. Whether you are doing a normal golf stroke or just putting, YOU CONTROL YOUR MOVEMENTS USING THE BODY AND NOT YOUR ARMS OR HANDS. Even if you find the tendency to let your natural feelings do otherwise, give your body time to get used to this. If you can achieve this you will have brought a certain sureness into your game to make it more enjoyable. And, you will be surprised just how many golfers there are, who reckon they possess so much feeling for the ball, but who produce very few successful results.

For the putt take your aim straight to the target i.e. the line of the feet and shoulders point to the hole (see Diagram 28a). The FACE OF THE PUTTER IS POINTING TOWARDS THE HOLE (SEE DIAGRAM 28B), AND, AT THE MOMENT WHEN THE BALL IS STRUCK THE CLUBHEAD IS ABOUT HALF AN INCH ABOVE THE GROUND (see Diagram 29). This is necessary so that the middle of the putter is aligned with the middle of the golf ball - (compare this with the fairway bunker shot later).

Just imagine the plane of a pendulum swinging. There are two equal zeniths and one nadir. The pendulum motion marks the segment of a circle. Try to swing your putter the same way, so that it moves backwards and forwards like the pendulum in a grandfather clock.

TIP 1   If you look at the position of the hands in Diagram 28a, you will note that they lie in a position directly under the ends of the shoulders. This is another advantage: the face of the putter is pointing always in the direction of the target as it oscillates. Thus the problem of a wrong position is avoided right from the start (see Diagram 30).

TIP2   If you strike the ball at such a point that the putter (pendulum) is rising again from the flat plane, the ball will roll more easily. This can be assured by placing the ball further to the left (see Diagram 31).

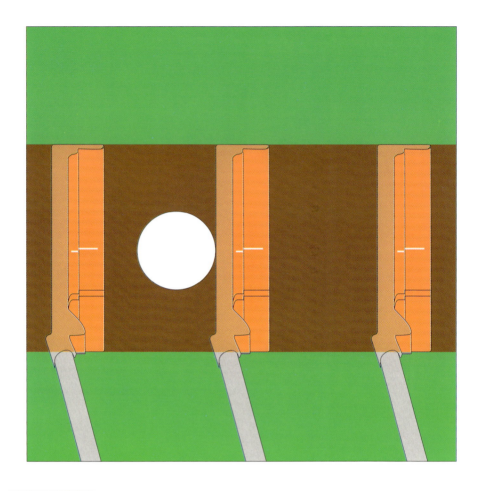

Diagram 30:
As it oscillates, the face of the putter is always pointing in the direction of the target.

70

Diagram 31:
The ball will roll more easily when it is struck on the upwards movement.

71

Diagram 32:
Chip: The weight is on the left, the hands distinctly in front of the ball.
The ball lies to the right in front of the right foot.

The Chip

Besides the putt, the chip is the stroke which is most likely to contribute towards producing a good score. If you can reach the green with a chip close to the hole (the expression used is "leaving it dead"), you will be able to down it with a putt. However a good tee-off stroke doesn't always mean that you have saved a stroke because there will be other strokes to make. Nevertheless, it will depend on how good an approach shot onto the flag has been played, whether the putt will be an easy one or not.

First, after you have been playing golf for quite a while, treat yourself to a "chipper" - a special club that is no more than a putter with a slightly higher-angled striking face (see Diagram 6 earlier). Accordingly, regarding the position of the ball, your address and your posture, you use the chip club in the same way as a putter. Thus in the shortest of time you can concentrate on the most important point of the chip shot - stroke distance. When you find out that you are playing successfully with this club, simply carry on.

When you have become more advanced as a golf player, you may find that you will prefer to use perhaps one of the other permissible 14 types of golf-clubs instead of this one, and you can dispense with it.

With the classic chip, with or without the special club, it is all about playing more of a flat trajectory shot in the direction of the hole. More than often this is the requirement when you are just off the green. Normally you can also use the putter for this shot. If the surrounds of the green consist of thick or long grass, you must 'fly' (chip) the ball onto the green, because the ball would be somewhat incalculably hindered in this type of area.

If you don't possess a "chipper", you can take a club with which you can reach the green in a single flight and it will roll out the rest of the way. As a rule this will be a 6,7,8 or 9-iron dependent on where your ball is lying. Generally speaking you can play a chip shot with any golf-club.

Diagram 33:
Chip: The wrists are stiff and the club accelerates through the ball.

For a chip with an iron, GRIP the club SHORTER than with a normal golf stroke, however the ball must be positioned almost OPPOSITE THE RIGHT foot. The feet and body are aimed more openly towards the target. Your WEIGHT is almost TOTALLY over the left foot. This will make sure that the BALL IS STRUCK BEFORE THE CLUB REACHES THE BOTTOM OF THE SWING. This effect will be accentuated since your hands are in front of the ball. If you draw a plumb-line from your grip to the ground it would fall some 10-15 inches in front of the ball (see Diagram 32).

Concerning the movements there are two points to note: Use the swing of your ARMS i.e. keep your WRISTS STIFF during the chip. Secondly, ACCELERATE the CLUB 'through' the ball with the follow through (see Diagram 33).

Success with the chip stands or falls with the finesse of the way you hit the ball. If you hit the ball cleanly it will land somewhere near the hole; for your own peace of mind this will be a good test as to whether your length and aim are well developed. If your positioning on the ball is as described above, you will soon be able to achieve a regular solid impact when chipping the ball.

Diagram 34:

Pitch: The ball lies in the middle, the hands are just in front of the ball, the weight is centred to the left and the aim is a little left of the target.

The Pitch

You will probably recognize the following situation: the ball lies in the middle of the fairway, but just in front of the flag there is a bunker. If you want to get on to the green there is only one way - a high shot which will come to a stop quickly. You have watched the pros on the television, who bring the ball to a rapid stop with such surety in such a situation - almost dreamlike. There are a number of reasons for this finesse, and they are not all to do with the player's prowess.

Just about any shot with the iron is principally a pitch. Let us describe a pitch under a distance of 100 yds for you. For this you would use normally a pitching wedge or sand wedge.

The steep angle (THE LOFT) OF THE CLUB IS WHAT MAINLY CAUSES THE BALL TO FLY HIGH UP IN THE AIR. The shot is played as normal e.g. the turn of the shoulders, the change of the centre of balance, and the position of the wrists always being correctly carried out. THE BALL LIES IN A POSITION ROUGHLY OPPOSITE THE CENTRE POINT BETWEEN THE FEET. The line-up of the feet and hips is turned slightly towards the target - in the open position (see Diagram 34). THE HANDS are positioned JUST IN FRONT OF THE BALL and YOUR WEIGHT is centred more over the LEFT LEG.

Try to carry out A FULL SWING. If you are aiming at a point some 50 yds ahead and you believe that the ball will go too far then grip the golf-club somewhat shorter.

You will create more spin over a distance, say of 50 yds, by using the shorter grip and a FULL SWING, than by attempting a half or three-quarter swing with a normal grip. This is because of the higher speed of the club as it swings. A part of this speed will be always converted into the distance achieved by the stroke, and a part into the backspin. So if the speed on the whole is higher, then the spin is stronger.

77

TIP When we talk about a „full swing", we don't mean you to take a wild swipe at the ball. You will very rarely be able to carry out an effective stroke when, for example, you are aiming for a short distance and you make a powerful stroke. In this situation, it is important that you swing the club smoothly and freely. This is what makes the difference. If you bear this in mind when addressing the ball, you will adjust your backswing automatically so that your smoothly and freely executed swing will lift the ball to the flag.

Do you want to bring your ball to a halt more quickly? Then you will have to use the modern materials which are on offer. In golf it is not only the choice of clubs that matters.

When you watch pro tournaments and observe a lot of strokes with backspin, there are two points to note. Of course the pros strike the ball very cleanly and this creates optimal spin. The pros are playing usually with a different type of ball (so-called Balata balls) which have more spin. Unfortunately these 3-piece balls are so soft, that when there is even the slightest hint of a poor stroke being played, they become immediately unusable. You meet a similar phenomenon in Badminton. When the shuttlecock has been slightly damaged by a poor shot, it is totally useless.

So-called "2-piece" balls are the ones usually used by novices. For several years now, 2-piece balls have been available, and these produce just as much spin as the pro's ball (3-piece). 2-piece balls are just as hardy and durable as the normal balls. Get one and go out and discover the rather lighter and softer sound this ball makes.

You will get to hear of a plethora of such possibilities and techniques which are not normally found by everyone. Ask your club pro about golf-balls - especially the ones that will take a lot of spin easily and still remain in one piece!

The rule for the novice is the same as the rule for the pro:
Spin = Control = Strength of Play = Fun

The Lob

If your ball is lying in a position only a short way away from the flag, but the green is hard, the spin achieved by the pitch will no longer be sufficient to bring the ball to a rapid halt.

In such a situation you will only be able to stop the ball by using a very steep trajectory - this is what the lob is used for. In the lob very little backspin is created at all over a short distance. This is equally so even if you use a particularly short grip.

It is all a question of the fact, that by playing the ball high up in the air, it falls back vertically to the ground, and thus will come to a halt quickly.

The pros also have special equipment for this shot. They use a so-called "lobwedge", which is a pitching wedge with a very high angled loft (approximately 60 degrees). This lends this club its name - "lofter".

We believe that you should forget about this club, because if you want to keep to the rule that you are only allowed to carry 14 clubs with you, you will very easily be able to decide on another club to use. In the last section of this book we give tips regarding suitable golf-club sets which will match each player's strength.

79

Diagram 35:
The face is opened wide.

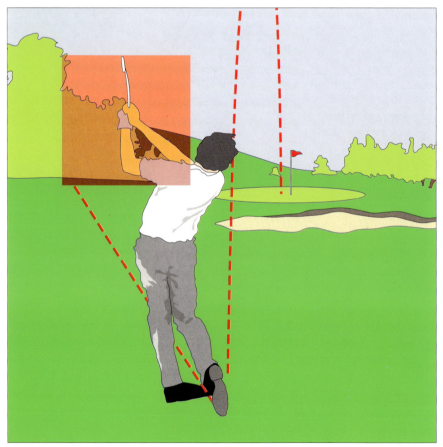

Diagram 36: Lob: The ball lies just to the left, the aim is way off to the left of the target, mainly the arms are used in the swing, and the club is accelerated through the ball.

80

You carry out the lob in the following manner:

Pick up your sand wedge and OPEN THE FACE - i.e. you twist the club in the hands so that the front edge of the striking area is pointing towards the target. Take up a position so that your feet, hips and shoulders are in line and aiming to the left of the target (see Diagram 35 & 36). Place the BALL down on a spot JUST TO THE LEFT of the centre point between your feet. When you now make a swing you must do the opposite - as an exception - to what normally constitutes a good golf stroke. Try to SWING USING THE ARMS AND HANDS. By doing this you create a higher angled impact with the ball and achieve a high trajectory. Be sure to ACCELERATE the club THROUGH THE POINT OF IMPACT WITH THE BALL.

DO NOT ATTEMPT - EVER - to try and strike the ball FROM UNDERNEATH - not even in this stroke. If you do it will always be a bad shot. You will either strike the ground or "top" the ball i.e. the ball is struck by the front edge of the clubface and not the full striking area. The club should move through the ball just as it was designed to do. The angle of attack (loft) is designed so that, together with the correct technique of the swing, a steep trajectory will be produced.

If the ground is particularly hard the sand wedge is not a suitable club for the lob because of its thick sole on the base (called "bounds"). You will be best off using the pitching wedge.

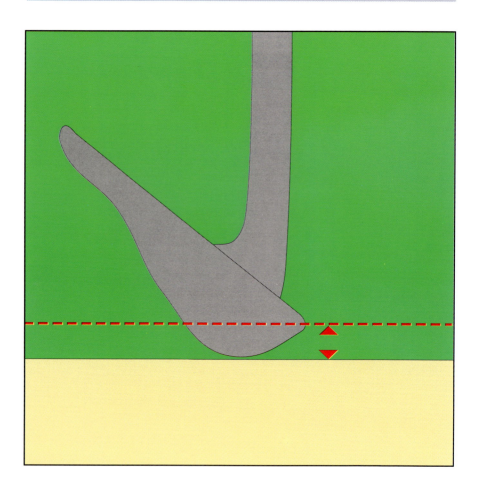

Diagram 37:

The front edge of the sand wedge sits up high because of the thick sole (bounds).

82

The Bunker Shot

With sand shots, near to the green, it is all about understanding what is happening. If you can work this out, you will be able to get the ball out of the bunker and consistently play onto the flag. One is always faced with a number of particularly difficult situations when trying to play out of the bunker. This creates a challenge to make the correct decision (i.e. play away from the hole and make sure you get out of the hazard) instead of blindly making an attempt at an impossible shot.

Take a good look at your sand iron. It is the only club in your bag where the LOWEST POINT of the sole of the club (bounds) is at the BACK EDGE. This means that when you set the head of the sand wedge down on the ground, the front edge is raised clearly higher (see Diagram 37). With your other irons this is not the case. The front and rear edges of the sole are at equal heights. This is why the sand iron is only suitable for shots outside the bunker when the ground is soft. Always check very carefully the "lie" of your ball and then decide whether you would prefer to use the sand iron or the pitching wedge.

In the bunker shot, the THICK SOLE (BOUNDS) of the sand wedge PREVENTS THE CLUB DIGGING TOO DEEPLY INTO THE SAND and becoming stuck.

On the contrary, if a good swing of the sand wedge strikes INTO THE SAND ABOUT AN INCH OR SO BEHIND THE BALL, it will have the energy to drag through the sand to the ball - at least in the surface sand area. The CLUB GLIDES THROUGH THE SAND AND THE BALL and appears in a 'bursting-out' cloud of sand. In other words it is NOT a question of HITTING THE BALL DIRECTLY, rather the club gathers up the ball and bursts through it (see Diagram 38).

83

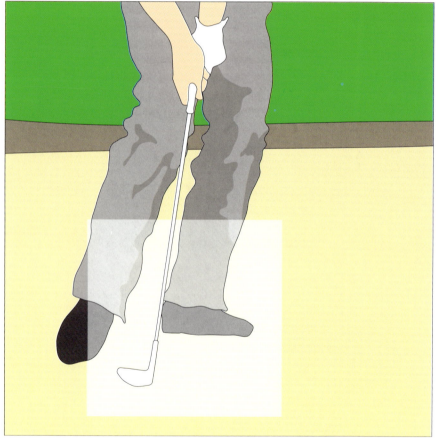

Diagram 38: The bunker shot: The golf-club strikes the sand first and then bursts through the ball.

84

In particular, IN SAND THE CLUB MUST BE SWUNG FAST as it glides through the ball, so that it doesn't become caught up in the sand. Sand creates a higher resistance than strokes in other ground types.

To back all this up, when addressing the ball, the club must be lightly twisted in the hands i.e. the face points to the right of the target. The BALL LIES to the LEFT OF CENTRE opposite the feet, which are placed OPEN and pointing in a direction well to the left of the target.

Training Exercise

a) First of all don't use a ball. Put the idea of a normal golf swing out of your mind. Pick up your sand iron and just imagine you are holding an axe and that you are going to chop up wood. You would lift the axe up vertically and not swing it back as in a golf swing. Now bring your sand wedge slowly up to your nose. Don't make a stroke but let it sink back down again. As you brought it up (unlike a backswing) you hardly needed to bend your left arm. It came right up simply by bending the wrists.

b) Bring the iron now up to your right ear and let it down again.

c) Next bring the iron up to your right shoulder and let it down again.

> d) Carry out points (a) - (c) again. This time, however, strike down hard with the club into the sand. Concentrate on guiding your "axe" more with the left arm and the left hand.
>
> At least when you carry out the stroke from the shoulder (see (c) above) the sand iron should burst a bit through the sand. With the other strokes (nose and ear) this probably would not be the case.
>
> e) Now carry out some bunker shots by striking behind the ball and into the sand. The movements practised in this exercise help you to swing the club back steeply and to let it sharply drop back again into the sand.

Don't worry that you may be swinging the club too steeply. When it comes to carrying out the shot you will almost automatically swing normally. This is why you should carry out this training exercise over and over again.

POSITION OF THE STRIKING FACE

When the SAND IS SOFT AND DEEP, you should OPEN the FACE more. If you are on hard sand - seldom the case on a golf-course - you need less of a 'burst' effect. In such situations, however, don't twist the club so much. Sometimes the sand is so hard that only the help of the pitching wedge will help you out of the sand. The sharp edge of this club will scrape into the top layer of the sand and burst into the ball.

THE AMOUNT OF SAND

The amount of sand to be moved determines the amount of resistance met by the club. If you aim well behind the ball, you will have to go through a lot of sand before you come to the ball. Because of this the ball will not receive a lot of inertia, and thus will not fly far from the bunker. In this way the club will still burst through to the ball, just as in any bunker shot, but there will be a larger amount of sand between the club and the ball at the moment of impact. The ball will receive no or hardly any spin and because of this will roll a long way on landing.

Using this technique you will only have a limited variety of control over the distance reachable. We can only recommend that all novices get to know all the different situations and types of sand consistencies. Above all for a short shot, aim more behind the ball than for a long shot. In both cases take a good swing through the ball (see Diagram 39). If necessary grip the club shorter.

THE STEEP ANGLED SHOT

For the advanced amongst you, we recommend an alternative more developed shot to the "axe" method. Use a steeper swing to ensure you that you strike the sand first. Everyone knows the feeling when the ball is struck "clean" and sails well over the green. Almost always you can get over this danger if you learn to take a steep swing when in the bunker. Little imperfections in the swing movement will not necessarily lead to a poor shot being made. This is because the clubhead lands further away from the ball with a steep swing, and is not swung through the ball. The design of the clubhead is the only reason why it eventually reaches the ball.

The angle of the shot will control and vary the distance the ball will go. This is, however, only a side effect. If you wish the ball to go a long way out of the bunker, you will need to make almost a normal backswing (i.e. less steep (see Diagram 40)). A flatter angled stroke with the club leads to less resistance and therefore a longer ball trajectory.

SPEED OF THE SWING

As a future golf player, you will gradually vary the force of your stroke through the ball automatically to match the distance you require to hit.

87

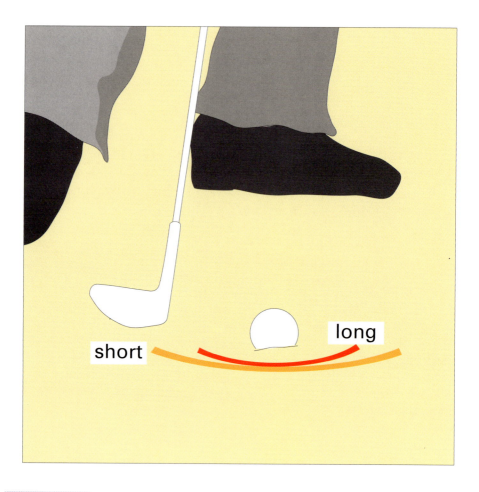

Diagram 39:
Little sand = less resistance = long shot
A lot of sand = lots of resistance = short shot

88

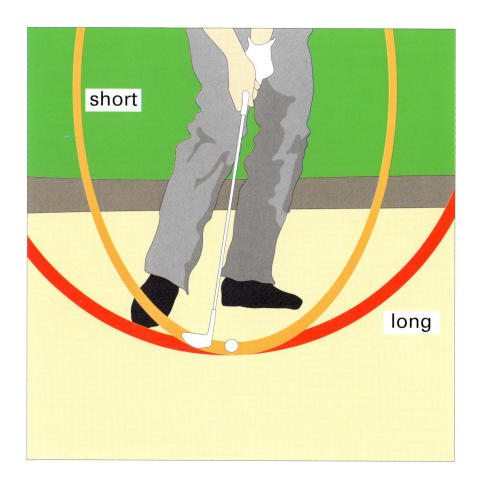

Diagram 40:
A steep swing is safer, but allows less distance than a flatter normal swing.

89

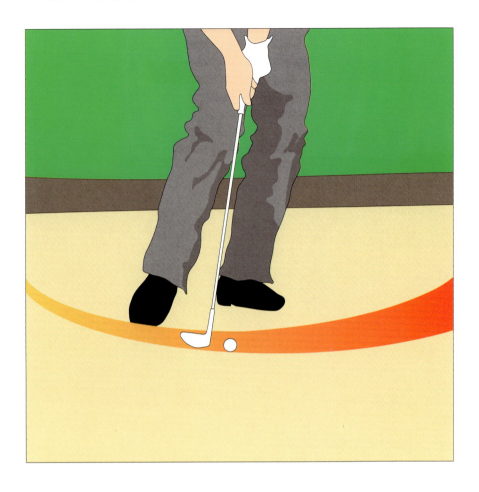

Diagram 41:
High swing speed = more safety = longer stroke distance

90

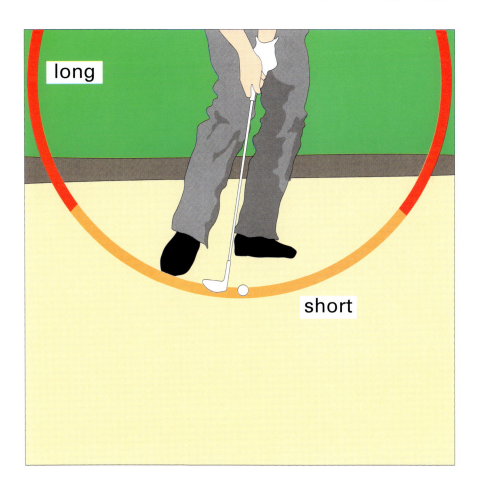

Diagram 42:
Longer swing = longer bunker shot
Short swing = short bunker shot

For short bunker shots you will automatically use a less dynamic swing than for a long one. Nevertheless, for short bunker shots you should also note that the club is accelerated as it passes through the ball (see Diagram 41). If you don't do this, the clubhead will not be correctly positioned at the moment of impact. Because you meet a strong resistance through the sand if the clubhead is not accelerated, this will cause an instability and lead to poor shots being made.

SWING LENGTH

The length of the swing is measured from the backswing to the follow through. When the swing length is made larger, the general rule is that the length of the shot will be greater. This is because the speed and the length of the backswing and the follow through are in direct proportion to each other. To achieve longer distances you must increase the speed of the club in the swing. For this you must swing the club further backwards i.e. take a longer "run-up" (see Diagram 42). On the other hand a longer backswing can also be of help for the short bunker shot as it will accelerate the clubhead through the ball.

You can try out all the various possibilities listed here one after the other until you decide which one you want to use. It is very likely that you will unintentionally end up with a varied combination of shots and this is also in order. The structure we have laid out above will serve as an orientation and aid to the causes and effects, and which, when understood will be decisive for your future performance. The principles of the bunker shot are valid and repeated in some form or other in the remainder of strokes in golf.

To summarise we reiterate: How far the ball will fly and roll is determined by the length of the swing - i.e. the height of the backswing and follow through - and the speed.

Difficult Situations

Now we would like to describe some technical tricks and dodges, so that you can master the difficult situations you will be confronted with during a round of golf. Since they crop up in most games to a certain extent, they will belong to the standard repertoire of your technique.

Unfortunately most hobby golfers do not know what course of action to take in such situations. So it really depends on understanding the correlation of the points, similar to the problem with the sand shot. Hobby golfers and novices alike are all able to learn the technical tricks of the trade to overcome these situations. We believe that a thorough understanding of the technical dodges will create a big step in your 'club-swinging' style and will make a genuine golfer out of you.

Diagram 43:
Long grass reduces the clubhead speed and ballspin.

94

Driving off the Rough

When you are driving the ball out of high grass (off the rough), you must consider first of all whether the position of the ball (the lie) even allows a shot to be taken. If you can hardly see the ball, it is advisable to declare the ball unplayable and take a penalty stroke instead. Although we do not want to dip into the rules of golf at this juncture, please note that this possibility is ALWAYS available to you, and in many cases this dodge will pay off.

If you decide to play the ball, be realistic about your choice of club. If you get the feeling that you could just about play the ball with a 4-iron, then choose a 6-iron. It will be worth it. Almost always you will hit the ball better using a shorter club, with the effect that it will go further than with a longer iron and bad ball impact.

GRIP the club, in addition, A LITTLE SHORTER and play the BALL from a stance RIGHT FROM CENTRE between your feet. THE MORE GRASS that comes in the way (see Diagram 43) means that you must move your stance SO THAT THE BALL LIES MORE TO THE RIGHT. Open the clubface (i.e. more to the right) - this is because when the club strikes the grass, the resistance met will close the angle on the face.

When executing the stroke, it is important that the club is brought down STEEPLY with a high angle to impact with the ball - remember the 'axe' training exercise in the bunker shot section (see Diagram 44). Please note that as an exception for this stroke, you must grip hard with the left hand, so that the club doesn't close too much at the moment of impact with the ball.

Also note that the ball will not spin very much, irrespective of how steeply you strike the ball, and, as a result will correspondingly roll a long way. If there is a hazard just in front of the green, you must accept that you

Diagram 44:

A steep angle of impact reduces the amount of grass between the club and the ball to a minimum.

96

will have to drop the ball short of the bunker ('lay up') thus having to play yet another stroke. An attempt to play the ball high ('carry') onto the green will, in most cases, end with the ball landing in the bunker. Should it actually gain the distance, it will go beyond the target and probably roll off the green.

The wood club shouldn't be considered in the rough - EVEN BY THE MOST CAPABLE - unless, that is, the ball is lying so cleanly as if it were on the fairway, or you are using a special club.

Driving out of the Fairway Bunker

This stroke demands more accuracy than a normal fairway shot. First of all you must also check to see if the position of the ball will permit you to make a full stroke. This will only be the case if the ball is lying cleanly on top of the sand, and when the sides of the bunker are not too steep. You must also ensure that the club you are going to use for the required distance, will create enough height to clear the sides of the bunker.

There are some golf-courses where the sand in the bunkers is so fine and deep that the ball always sinks into it, when it comes to a rest. In soft sand this is merely caused by the weight of the ball itself. In this case it is not worth trying to do a normal stroke. We describe special stroke techniques for such a case in Part 2.

If the BALL is lying on the surface, address it so that it is in a position JUST TO THE RIGHT OF CENTRE of the line of the feet. Note that your feet will sink down into the sand a little, and therefore in order to compensate for this you must take A SHORTER GRIP. This in turn will

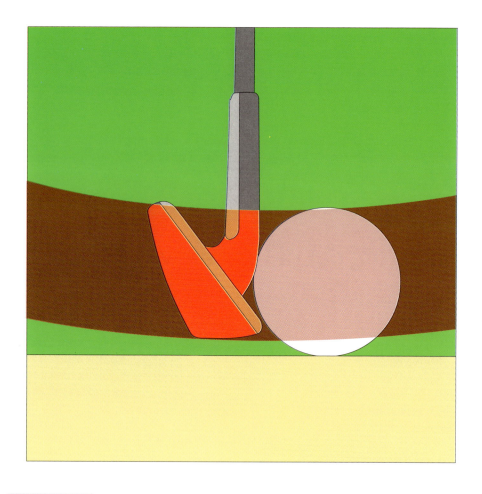

Diagram 45:
Fairway bunker shot: The club does not touch the sand, but is still struck fully.

reduce the length of the stroke, and this also must be compensated for by the choice of the club.

The most important factors on such a surface are a FIRM STANCE AND GOOD BALANCE. During your swing the ground will give way under you a little - be prepared for this. Thus your address should be made a little more 'compact'. Moreover you should use a CLUB A NUMBER higher - e.g. use a No.6 instead of a No.7. This will give you a better balance and you will be able to SWING MORE SMOOTHLY and concentrate on hitting the ball better.

You can be sure that your ball will hardly move out of the bunker let alone 'fly' any distance if you touch or strike the sand in front of the ball.

Just imagine the parabola that your clubhead moves through. When the ball is hit at exactly the lowest point on the curve, and there has been nearly no contact with the sand at all, then it will be cleanly struck (see Diagram 45).

TIP   In order to give this shot the necessary accuracy it must deserve, we recommend that you fix your eyes on a spot on the ball where you initially want to make impact.

99

Diagram 46: Uphill position: The line of the shoulders adapts to the line of the slope. The body weight is moved uphill during the follow through. The ball flies higher and shorter. The ball lies just to the left of centre.

100

Slope Shots

Other than on very few golf-courses you will always find places where the ball is lying on a slope. This means, that irrespective of your position on the course, YOUR ADDRESS MUST BE ADAPTED TO THE SLOPE. According to which way the slope is running, your left leg and foot could be lower than your right (called the 'downhill' position), or vice versa (called the 'uphill' position). Alternatively the ball could be higher than your feet (called 'standing below the ball'), or lower than your feet (called 'standing above the ball').

UPHILL

In this position it is very often the case that you cannot see the target. Walk a few paces forward until you are sure that you are not going to hit anyone with your shot, and, note a point on the ground over which you will want to aim the ball.

Position your SHOULDERS so that they are PARALLEL TO THE SLOPE. You can check this easily by holding a club out in front of you. If the club is pointing into the slope instead of being parallel to the ground then the lowest point of the swing will not exactly reach the ball and it will hardly be struck cleanly. Your eyes will tend to be influenced in the same way as a result, because THE HEAD TIPS TO THE RIGHT TOGETHER WITH THE SHOULDERS and adapt themselves to the line of the ground. Adopt a good balance by taking-up a relatively BROAD ADDRESS. Play the ball from a position JUST TO THE LEFT OF CENTRE between your feet.

In the swing itself pay attention to keeping the RIGHT KNEE STILL, since when you start the backswing the weight of your body is pushed forcibly downhill. By the same dint, such as when taking a swing on the level, by letting the knee give, you will not be able to coil up the tension in

Diagram 47: Downhill position: The line of the shoulders adapts again to the line of the slope. The body weight is moved uphill during the backswing. The ball lies just to the right of centre. The ball goes further with a lower trajectory.

102

your muscles. Even more importantly you must concentrate fully on MOVING THE BODY WEIGHT UPHILL (see Diagram 46). The stroke ends with your balance fully over the left leg. Take care not to let your body weight fall back onto your right leg at the end of the swing.

When you are practising the uphill shot, you will find out that in moving the body weight uphill, it is more a question of keeping your balance than putting power into your stroke.

From this position your BALL WILL FLY HIGHER and will LAND A LITTLE SHORTER. Therefore take club a NUMBER MORE e.g. a 6-iron rather than a No.7.

DOWNHILL

In principle you carry out the downhill shot in exactly the same way. The only thing is that you will now stand so that the ball is OPPOSITE THE CENTRE of your feet or perhaps slightly to the left of the centre line of your feet. Bend your SHOULDERS so that they are again PARALLEL TO THE SLOPE, and make sure that also your head moves with them.

This time, during the BACKSWING, you must get the body weight to move uphill, with the weight transferring to the right leg. BE CAREFUL HOW YOU USE THE BODY WEIGHT because it will automatically want to fall back down the slope. Here again you will have to practice your ability to retain your BALANCE DURING THE MOVEMENTS. Note that the ball will fly lower and will roll out longer than for a normal stroke on the level. Normally you will USE A CLUB NUMBER LESS e.g. a 7-iron instead of a 6-iron (see Diagram 47).

STANDING ABOVE THE BALL

When the position of the feet is higher than the ball, you are standing 'above' the ball. Be aware during your aim that, as a rule, the ball, when struck, will curve off a little to the right. This is caused by the steepness of

Diagram 48:

Standing above the ball: The weight is centred more over the ankles, the hands are clear of the legs. The address is a little to the left of the target because the ball will turn to the right.

the swing plane. You will learn why a steep swing plane tends to cause a faint "slice" in the section about the 'slice'.

Play the BALL from a position just to the LEFT OF CENTRE opposite your feet. Place the CLUBHEAD FLAT on the sloping ground so that the tip is not sticking up. When you now lean into the ball be sure to take up quite a broad address and that your WEIGHT is positioned more ON THE ANKLES (see Diagram 48).

If you find it difficult to balance certain parts of the body over your feet, carry out the following training exercise:

Training Exercise Close your eyes and try to get the feel where your main weight lies. Switch your centre of balance from one ball of the foot to the other, and then onto the ankles, and then also onto the outsides of your feet. Finally put your weight on your ankles and leave it there. This exercise will help you to orientate yourself on your feet.

When you are standing 'above' the ball, you will have plenty of room to swing, but make sure that your HANDS are well AWAY FROM THE BODY. It can occur, otherwise, that there is not enough room to swing past the knees. At the same time, this takes care of the point that the club should be lying cleanly on the ground.

With the swing, balance is again the important point. If you are going to lose your balance this will nearly always mean you topple forward down the slope. Try to avoid this and RESTRAIN YOUR SWING so as to always keep your balance.

Diagram 49:

Standing below the ball: The weight is more over the balls of the feet. The club is gripped shorter, the ball goes to the left - hence the aim is more towards the right of target.

106

STANDING BELOW THE BALL

If you have been following the principles of the slope shot you will already know what to do for this:

In order to be able to adopt a position at the normal distance away from the ball, PULL YOURSELF UP as far as necessary - your feeling will tell you when you are right. You can also take a SHORTER GRIP on the CLUB. You will have to do this in order to set the clubhead flat on the ground, dependent on the gradient of the slope. Note, however, that a shorter grip leads to a shorter distance achieved. Also the ball will fly off to the left - again see the next section as to why. You must therefore aim a little to the right (see Diagram 49).

Stand with your weight more on the balls of the feet and maintain your balance during the swing.

107

Special Strokes

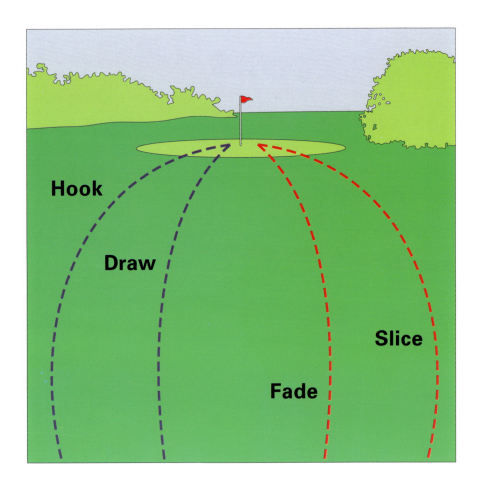

The various trajectories - Slice; Fade; Draw and Hook

108

The Slice

You will find situations, when it can be very useful to be able to play the ball in a curve rather than straight ahead.

While the 'slice', seen from the player's perspective, starts from the left or from straight ahead and curves sharply off to the right, the 'fade' begins by going straight and then curves slightly off to the right. The 'fade' is therefore called the controlled "small slice".

Pros often select the fade as the trajectory for their iron shots onto the flag since it characteristically has a higher trajectory and rolls to a stop quicker than the 'draw' (see Diagram 50). The flight path from left to right is created by the sidespin applied to the ball at the moment of strike.

IN ORDER TO ACHIEVE SPIN THERE MUST BE NO IMPEDIMENTS IN THE WAY BETWEEN CLUB AND BALL SUCH AS GRASS, OR WATER, otherwise the ball will slip on the striking face and will not take the spin (cf., Diagram 51). This factor plays quite a role in pro golf tournaments. For these the grass is mown very short, they use softer balls, which take more spin (see section on Pitch), and they attempt to reduce the disturbance created by any impediment lying in their way to a minimum by using a steep high-angled stroke (i.e. the club is brought down steeply from a high backswing onto the ball - (see section on Bunker Shots)).

As a rule the ball will go in the direction in which the clubface is pointing. The main factor is the underside edge of the face.

Naturally the trajectory will be influenced by the direction in which the club is swung as well. If the clubface is pointing to the right of the target, but the club is swung to the extreme left of the target, the ball will begin its flight left from the target. It is exactly within this framework that the ball is given its spin which will take it to the right.

Diagram 51: Slice: The club is pointing towards the target. The aim is towards the left of the target. The swing is carried out normally along the line of aim.

The direction of the clubface is determined by the address position of the player. If he aims with the line of his feet, hips and shoulders to the left of the target, then it follows that the swing will be made in that direction.

As seen from the player's perspective, the club creates the spin on the slice as the face is opened at the moment of the strike (e.g. when it points to the right). If the clubface is pointing hard to the right, the ball will curve hard to the right also; the less it is pointing off to the right the less it moves to the right.

The Intentional Slice Shot

First of all aim with your club at the TARGET (e.g. the flag). Now stand with the line of your FEET, HIPS AND SHOULDERS CLEARLY POINTING TO THE LEFT. If you were to execute a NORMAL SWING, the ball would fly off along the line of your feet (left of the target) and then would turn towards the right in the direction of where the clubface was originally pointing. For this the ball is in a POSITION SLIGHTLY LEFT of centre between your feet (see Diagram 51).

The fade is played in a similar way. Feet, hips and shoulders are pointing a little less towards the left. The 'blade' (clubface) is only slightly opened.

When playing a fade you must take note of two effects. First of all the ball will FLY HIGHER and secondly it will LAND A LITTLE EARLIER. With the clubface opened more - relative to your address - a greater attack angle is created. So you could say that in this way a 6-iron has become a No.7 iron. Therefore take a CLUB ONE HIGHER for this shot.

Diagram 52: Hook: The club is pointing at the target. The aim is towards the right of the target. The position of the clubhead must be ignored. The swing is carried out along the line of the aim.

112

The Hook

All the factors applicable to the slice apply in the opposite direction for the hook. The hook's "little brother" is the 'draw'. Pros often use this stroke for their tee-shot. The draw flies a little flatter than the fade and rolls further. The sidespin on the ball causes the curve in flight in the slice and hook. We know the aerodynamic principle of this from football, just as when a player shoots a goal by curving the ball in from the corner flag. The biomechanical term for this is the "Magnus effect".

In football it is the position of the feet which is important - in golf it is the position of the striking face at the moment of impact with the ball. If the striking face is pointing to the left of the target then the ball will go in that direction - unless of course the point of aim of the club is not running in the same direction.

If the player swings his club in a direction to the right of the target, but the striking face is pointing directly towards the target, or even to the left of it, then the ball will be spun strongly and this creates a hook shot.

Again the direction of movement is determined by the aim of the player. He will swing the club in the direction in which the line-up of his feet, hips and shoulders is pointing.

The less there is a difference in direction between the aim of the striking face and the body, it will mean, as a general rule, that the flight curvature will also be less. If the aim of the striking face and the direction of the body are the same, and the swing is constant along the line of the body, then you will see a normal stroke produced.

113

The Intentional Hook Shot

Aim the club again exactly at the TARGET. Place your FEET (and HIPS and SHOULDERS) so that they are CLEARLY POINTING IN A DIRECTION TO THE RIGHT OF the target. Just ignore the position of your club and make a SWING ALONG THE LINE OF YOUR FEET. The BALL is lying on a spot JUST TO THE LEFT OF CENTRE opposite and between your feet (see Diagram 52).

At the moment of impact with the ball, the club will stay closed in relation to your stance. The ball will start off along the approximate line of your feet (i.e. to the right) and will then curve sharply to the left.

Because the club tends to 'lose' its angle by virtue of the closed position of the striking face (as seen from the player's perspective), the ball will FLY FLATTER AND ON THE WHOLE FURTHER. It will also roll out longer than a normal shot. The long roll-out is used by the pros to increase their distance when teeing-off (see above). Therefore when doing the hook, choose for example a 6-iron instead of a 5-iron.

The reason why the majority of golfers find difficulty with intentional curve shots isn't because of their own technical inability. The technical intricacies are practically the same as those for a normal stroke. The slice and hook should be just as easily carried out with the same success or failure rate as any normal stroke.

The fact that this is not always the case has its roots in the simple problem, that it is difficult for all of us to ignore either the wide open position of the striking face (Slice), or its closed position (Hook) and at the same time take-up a different address to normal. In order to train for this capability - we call it 'mirror inversion training' - we suggest the following exercise.

Training Exercise

First of all check your grip. It will be correct (neutral) if, when addressing the ball, you can see 2-3 knuckles of the left hand, and the 'V' between the thumb and the forefinger points approximately to the right shoulder or to the left of it.

Now check your address position. It will be neutral if the line of your feet, hips and shoulders points towards the target or just slightly left of it. (Lay a club down along the line of the feet, hips and shoulders and ask a friend to check it for you). A good aid to all this is to use a video camera to check. You can also go through the routine with your club pro. Otherwise simply get a friend to do the checking as we have said.

a) In your mind's eye, pick out a spot (target) on the ground. Take your putter without a ball and take-up an address position aiming clearly to the right of the target (- the line of the feet, hips, shoulders, and the putter as well, are all pointing to the right).

b) Grip the putter as if you were going to putt and (without using a ball) let it swing like a pendulum along your line of aim.

c) Now, still swinging the putter, try to turn it in your hands so that the striking face points at the target (i.e. to the left). Keep the putter swinging along the line of your feet. It is important to note that you should NOT turn the putter WITH your hands, BUT IN your hands.

d) Take hold of a 7-iron. Other than the address and the grip, which should now be as for a normal golf stroke, do the same as in (a) and (b) above. Aim the club and the body clearly to the right of the target and carry out the swing along this line. Carry out a half swing and remain relaxed.

e) Now, WHILST STILL swinging like a pendulum, turn the club more and more in your hands so the striking face ends up pointing at the target. YOUR SWING, BACKWARDS AND FORWARDS, MUST STILL BE ALONG THE LINE OF THE FEET!

f) Repeat (e) above again. When you have turned the striking face to point at the target, relax your grip to be as light as possible and concentrate on the weight of the clubhead.

g) Place your club down to point at the target from the beginning. Position yourself to aim clearly to the right. Your swing should now not be as much as before.

h) Repeat (g) above, but this time swing backwards and forwards a little more. Keep your grip relaxed and concentrate on the clubhead. When you reach the point that you can 'feel' the clubhead at every swing, start using a ball. It will curve away to the side.

i) Now do a full swing, adopting your address as before. Make the swing along your aim. The ball will now curve quite sharply to the left.

You can carry out this exercise to train for the slice as well - but with the ball moving off to the other side.

Repeat the exercise from time to time. Each time check your grip and your position while addressing the ball.

Gradually your body will learn to adapt itself naturally and ignore the club. The key to it is that slowly you build-up your swing speed without losing your 'feel' for the golf-club. The club must always be swung along the line of your aim (feet, hips and shoulder line).

116

The Swing Plane

Using the expression "plane", becoming now more popular to describe the swing, it allows us to illustrate the propensities of the ball's flight and trajectory in a simple manner. Just imagine a gigantic gramophone record which is placed over the head and rests on the shoulders and with its edge resting on the ground. The golf player is bent slightly forward with his arms on the underside of the record and his head is looking down at the ball (see Diagram 53).

In an ideal golf swing, it is the player's shaft which determines the swing plane. Scientists, studying biomechanics, have established that there are actually several different plane levels. We shouldn't worry about this because golf players try to be economical with their exertions, and try to use only ONE plane level. The subconscious will only recognize that there is one plane level, and will use this.

If the swing plane is lined up to the left of the target, one also uses the expression "from-the-outside-in", and the striking face is straight and lined up with the feet, this will induce a 'slice'.

If the swing plane is lined up to the right of the target - one speaks now of "from-the-inside-out" - then with the striking face straight, a 'hook' will be induced.

In Diagram 53, the swing plane is parallel to the player, and if the ball is struck cleanly, this plane will result in a straight shot.

If you consider the case of a short player, the plane will lie flatter and his club will move faster towards the "inside". It will be easier to induce a hook in such a case. The swing plane for a short player is extremely similar to the characteristics of playing a shot 'standing below the ball'. On the other hand, when the ball is lying lower than the feet (such as with a tall person), there will be a more steeply aligned plane created, which will make the fade or the slice easier to execute.

117

Diagram 53:

The taller the player the steeper the plane. In a steep plane, as illustrated here, the club will be moved less from the 'inside' than in a flat plane.

Divots

Have you had a close look at the grass that sits around your golf ball? At this juncture we would like to explain, where and why, you should be scraping a lump of grass out of the ground when you hit the ball!

In order to hit the ball cleanly, apart from a few exceptions, it should be positioned opposite your feet and the clubhead should impact with the ball while it is still on the downstroke.

Shortly after the ball has absorbed the energy from the clubhead and begins to move away from it, the club will scrape into the ground as it reaches the lowest part of the swing and a lump of grass will be cut away (see Diagram 54).

How much and how thick this is depends on the individual swing. It is important, however, that your 'divot' is always cut out from the point where the ball starts to move away from the clubhead i.e. behind the ball. It is also interesting to examine the way the divot has been cut out. From the small rectangular scrape hole you can establish in what way and direction the club struck the ball. If the plane of the swing was straight, the divot will be pointing at the target.

If your club came in from the outside, the divot will point to the left - if it came in from the inside it will point to the right. In this manner you will always be able to check and control your plane.

Should your divot indicate that the outside tip of the clubhead went deeper into the ground than the shaft end of the blade, you will be able to deduce that you have brought the club down too vertically onto the ball (see Diagram 55). In such a case you should check your address position. It is also possible that the lie angle of your club is too flat (see Diagram 7 earlier).

If the divot indicates a deeper cut on your side of the clubhead blade, rather than on the edge away from the body (see Diagram 56), then your club is perhaps too long, or, you are not resting the of the club sole on the ground when you take up the address position - or the lie angle is too steep (again compare Diagram 7).

119

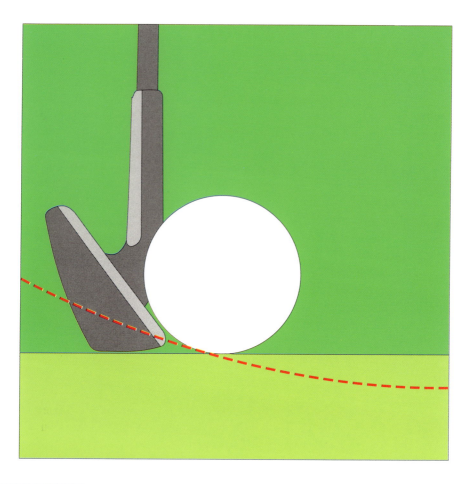

Diagram 54:

The divot is the lump of grass that is cut from the ground by the blade of the club (iron) immediately after the moment of impact with the ball

120

Diagram 55:
Divot is too deep at the toe.

Diagram 56:
Divot is too deep at the heel.

Driving into the Wind

The first point to note is that WHEN THERE IS A REALLY STRONG WIND, you can add at least ANOTHER TEN STROKES TO THE HANDICAP. So, for example, if your handicap is 36 and after nine holes you are 25 over par this will be quite normal. Even in pro tournaments the average score in strong windy conditions will increase by at least five strokes. Recognition of these realistic and limiting estimates will allow you to play your game in a little more relaxed manner.

When you address the ball, use a broader-based address and position the ball a little more to the right so that you will strike it at the earliest possible moment. Do not try to hit the ball too hard - keep your swing smooth and fluid. Position yourself on the FAIRWAY with the ball at a point RIGHT OF CENTRE opposite your feet. Position your hands and grip SOME 8-12 INCHES IN FRONT OF THE BALL. By doing this you give your club less loft - a No 7-iron becomes a 5- or a 4-iron (see Diagram 57). With your hands so far in front of the ball, you will be able to come down more easily onto it with a steeper-angled stroke.

The address, described above, will only be of use to you, if you have your hands positioned in front of the ball at the moment of impact (see Diagram 58). This movement and action is perhaps the most difficult to execute in golf. You will only be able to practice it and get the right feel for it actually in windy conditions. It is also necessary that you USE A LIGHT GRIP on the club in order to be able to 'feel' the weight of the club-head. For a slight headwind use a club TWO numbers higher, and in a strong headwind THREE or even FOUR numbers higher than normal. Don't exaggerate your swing. A 'QUIET' SWING will permit better impact with the ball, and, moreover a flatter trajectory will be achieved.

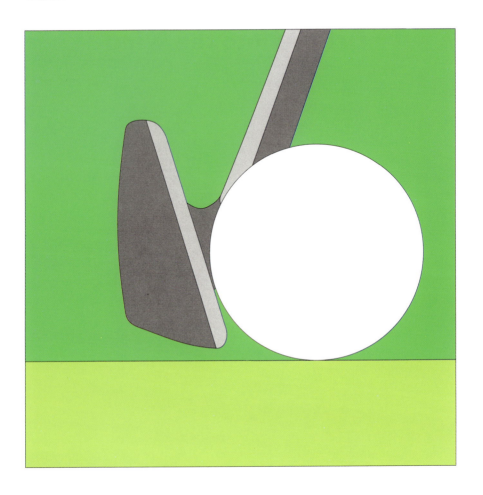

Diagram 57:
View of the position of the striking face on the ball if the hands are in front of the ball.

Diagram 58:
 Into the wind: If the hands and lower body are in front of the ball at the moment of impact, the result will be a flat trajectory.

125

Diagram 59:

Tail wind: The hands and body are behind the ball, the club strikes the ball on the upwards movement and lifts it high into the air.

126

Driving with a Following Wind

For this situation you also need to adopt a broad address posture, and position the ball opposite the left foot. Hold the club in a light grip so that you are able to 'feel' the clubhead as you swing. Don't be put off by the sound of the wind. Use a club one to three less than normal. Make sure your swing is smooth and watch how you maintain your balance. Try to ensure that your hands and body are behind the ball at the moment of impact (see Diagram 59). In this way the loft of the club will be increased. Using a 5-iron you will produce a trajectory as if it were a 6- or 7-iron. This will mean that with a following wind, greater distances will be reached. Please note that despite the high trajectory, the ball will roll on as it lands.

Part Two

Mistakes and Correcting the Basics

HOW TO IMPROVE YOUR GRIP

The only contact you have with the club as a player is with the hands i.e. the grip. Through the medium of your hands you get the feel of the club. You can feel its weight, tell whether it is a ladies' or man's club, whether it is a wood or an iron and what kind of grip it has - leather or rubber. All this comes from the hands without you needing to look at the club. Try it out - the difference between a wood and an iron will surprise you; the wood is considerably LIGHTER than an iron.

The important characteristics of a correct grip are as follows:

With the club in your hands you must be able to move your hands and wrists freely. You should not be gripping too hard. Your grip will be too strong if you can see white areas building around your fingers. The blood circulation is prevented by the fingers gripping too hard. Your hands must sit 'neutrally ' on the club i.e. your hands grip the club in a natural position as they hang down from the body. The 'neutral' position, together with a light grip, will allow the hands to move in any direction. When you swing, the clubhead will pull against the wrists, which themselves follow the movement of the body.

Now how can you establish whether your grip is neutral or not (see Diagrams 60, 61 and 62)?

First of all you will find in Straight Golf Part 1 a comprehensive training exercise for adopting the correct grip, and which told you how to compare the position of your hands on the club. In addition to this, you must control your grip during the swing. You can best do this by noting your follow through at the end of your swing - your 'finish'.

Diagram 60:
The 3-knuckle grip

Diagram 61:
The 2-knuckle grip

132

Diagram 62:
The 4-knuckle grip

133

> **TIP** If, at the end of the swing, the club is positioned in your hands exactly as it was in the address position, then you need not worry any further.

If, however, the position of your fingers or your hands has changed in the meanwhile, then you have a problem with your grip. Also, if you need to apply a lot of pressure, or the opposite, or need to let go of the club, simply because you are not in a position to keep hold of it at the end of the swing, then you need to examine carefully what is wrong with your grip.

As a reminder: You have got the right grip, if;
... you can see 2-3 knuckles of the left hand;
... you can see a 'V' between the thumb and the forefinger of both hands;
.... the 'V's' point approximately to the right shoulder;
... the end of the grip is protruding a little out of the left hand;
... the club is lying more in the fingers than in the palm of the hand.

You will very quickly be able to determine that the 'finish'-method is quite useful to recognize and evaluate how your grip is in comparison to the "perfect grip".

When you have to correct your grip, it will not be easy to feel comfortable with the new CORRECT position of your hands. Your hands will not accept the new points of pressure and they will try anything to stray back to the old points. This usually manifests itself in the fingers fidgeting around, trying to find an acceptable position.

This is where the pros have their strength - they have learned to accept unusual feelings and despite these still execute good shots. The trajectory of the ball will be the living proof of the correctness of the change undertaken. It is exactly such fortitude of mind, which is the factor, above all others, that leads to an improvement in training. If there is any particular point which decides a good player from a bad one, then it is the way in which a successful golfer will rigorously put into practice changes in their technique, and by doing so avoid any unnecessary movement.

For those who wish to make an improvement we recommend they practice this. Since, however, you are not yet a playing professional, let us suggest a further possibility for you to be able to improve your grip:

Training Exercise

a) Take hold of a 7-iron and grip it normally.

b) Stretch out both of your little fingers and your two forefingers as well as the right thumb (see Diagram 63).

c) Now hit 20-30 balls.
You will only be able to do this if the club is sitting in your hands in a 'neutral' position. If the clubface was closed or open by the end of this exercise it would be exactly in the middle i.e. 'neutral'. You will always now grip the club automatically in a neutral position - otherwise you would not be able to move freely, or not even be able to hold it. Sometimes the club will even turn into the correct position on its own (see Diagram 64).
N.B. Even the weakest Senior Ladies player will be able to do this exercise.

Diagram 63:
The Ben Hogan-Grip

136

Diagram 64:
The club automatically moves correctly.

HOW TO IMPROVE YOUR POSTURE

Let it be said from the beginning: We reckon that the most difficult and at the same time the most important point to master, for a solid basis of your technique, is the optimum stance for the address.

A good address is characterised by good balance in combination with the right amount of relaxation (or tenseness) in the muscles which come into play. From Straight Golf Part I you will already know from the diagrams how this position should look. It is all a question of only using the muscles that you need to adopt an upright position. All of your other muscles will act as a brake to the action of your golf swing if they are tense.

Everyone is built differently. In order to have good balance for the swing, someone who has short legs will stand differently than someone who has long legs. Some players have longer arms - some a fat tummy.

Thus with differing body sizes, the stance will consist of different positions in relation to the ball. The club pros speak of *body angles* in this context. So, how do you discover which address will match your body size?

Let's look at the wrong positions depicted in Diagrams 65, 66 and 67. If you can only half-recognize yourself, then carry out the following training exercise for the address, which we have worked up for all body types.

Diagram 65:
The wrong address - knees locked back

139

Diagram 66:
The wrong address - player is sitting back.

Diagram 67:
The wrong address - the chin is on the chest and the back is humped.

141

Training Exercise

a) Stand side-on to a mirror so that you can look at the side of your body.

b) Stand upright and slip your hands behind your back - like a teacher does.

c) Drop into the 'skiing' position - like 'Eddie the Eagle' (see Diagram 68).

d) Just imagine you are doing a ski-jump and you are moving down the slide, just about to jump - gradually lift your body into the 'jump' (see Diagrams 69a/69b).

e) Notice how your knees remain exactly underneath your armpits, irrespective of how upright your body has moved.

f) Somewhere, just short of completely standing-up, there is the spot where you would be able to stand with your arms relaxed in front of you with the club, so that its underside is flat on the ground. This is the optimum address position (see Diagram 70). You will now have maximum balance in relation to your anatomy.

This training exercise works because you can only stand upright if you are standing over the middle of your feet. Likewise, just like the address position, your rear is pushed slightly backwards as your body leans forward - otherwise you would lose your balance. Simultaneously, by virtue of adopting the imaginary ski-jumper position, your backbone is tensed enough to hold your upright position steady.

Diagram 68:
In the 'skiing' position balance is maintained.

143

Diagram 69a:

Moving to the upright position ...

Diagram 69b:
... your knees remain exactly underneath your shoulders.

Diagram 70:
With your arms relaxed in front of you, gripping the club, you obtain the optimum address position.

146

HOW TO IMPROVE YOUR AIM

Regularly check whether you are standing in the direction of the target. Take special note of the line-up of your hips and shoulders, because it is not the feet alone which determine the direction of the swing which you eventually make.

Training Exercise

a) Ask a friend to lay golf clubs down on the ground around your address position to represent the direction of your feet, hips and shoulders.

b) Now leave your address position and step back and look at the differing directions in which the clubs are pointing.

c) You will be able to see an exact idea of the direction in which your body is pointing.

This method is a very good way to check your aim. Additionally you can make a video, but you will mostly only see your hips and shoulders. On the other hand you will see the picture in three dimensions e.g., both your shoulders and hips.

During your game your body will invariably adopt differing positions. The ability to be able to aim always at the target does not necessarily depend on your capability to orientate yourself. Each person has developed different characteristics as he has grown up. There are golfers who already have sufficient perception of their own environment that they do not need to look at the target. Such people simply 'feel' their position and aim correctly. However, very few of us possess such a sensitivity to be able to orientate ourselves so that a correct aim is always guaranteed.

For the majority of golfers the recommendation is therefore to develop a pre-shot routine which will permit a correct aim. This routine becomes the most important point in the preparation prior to every stroke.

147

The fact that practically every successful pro in the world has such a preparation routine serves to emphasize this point. Good players can repeat the routine exactly the same, each time, down to the fraction of a second.

A good example of this is perhaps the decisive putt by Bernhard Langer in the 1993 Ryder Cup - the most important team tournament in the world played between Europe and the USA. For his part everything hung on the last game between him and Hale Irwin. Langer had to win each of the last holes in order to still have a chance. As the whole of the golfing world looked on whilst he shaped up to the two-and-a-half yard putt, he gave himself time and studied the putting line carefully. Then he stood behind the ball and rehearsed his putt down to the last millimetre, just like he does for each putt he makes. The timing of his preparation was within a tenth of a second of the same time he takes for every putt. Although the putt missed, he knew exactly that he had done everything correctly.

The routine which takes about 20 seconds has an inner rhythm which combines all the various steps - lining up, aiming and the swing. Since the actual movement of the putter (also the same in a normal golf swing) only lasts one to two seconds, this is not so important. There are actually a number of other movements and steps which are combined and belong to the putt (or shot).

Once the essential movement has been embedded into a sequence of laid down steps, one will have a firm framework, which gives you a feeling of enormous security. If your routine is always the same then the pressure one feels in carrying out a shot will be much less and the swing more relaxed and better.

All this leads to Bernhard Langer winning the second Masters title in the Spring of the same year (1993) i.e. before the Ryder Cup.
It would bring him also a very successful Winter season with the World Pro Championship.

The point about all this, we argue, is, that if Bernhard Langer were to change his pre-shot routine prior to every important stroke, he would not only have NOT holed his Ryder Cup putt, he would not have won either the Masters nor the World Pro Championship. This pre-shot routine, as we have already said, is followed by practically all the pros. The consequence of Bernhard Langer following his routine steadfastly, on good days as well as bad, is unique and surely a cornerstone of his successful career.

The following training exercise for your personal routine is once again recommended, and should be blended into your habits to complement them. It will only serve its purpose if you use it for every golf stroke you play, whether it is on the fairway or on the driving range.

Training Exercise

a) Stand at least three paces behind the ball.

b) Decide how you are going to play the ball. Take the club loosely in the right hand with the weight of the club resting on the ground.

c) Move forward to the ball and as you do switch your eyes backwards and forwards from the ball to the target. The club is still resting loosely in the right hand.

d) Place the club cleanly behind the ball with your right hand, and line it up with the lower part of the blade pointing in the direction of the target.

e) Look at the target and then at the clubface. Adopt your address position and line up your feet. The club is still lying loosely in the fingers of the right hand.

f) Before you do your backswing, grip the club now calmly with both hands. The grip and the backswing should mould into one flowing movement.

149

What happens when you deliberately stand behind the ball? Before you carry out your stroke you are automatically taking stock of the situation, the conditions and the environment you are in. You can see the target. You see the ball and formulate in your mind the address position that you will assume (see Diagram 71).

It is particularly important that you are at least three paces behind the ball and not less. At this distance you are able to assimilate the spatial conditions and information necessary to judge the length of the shot you are about to make. Also, the action of switching your eyes from ball to target as you move forward (see Diagram 72) gives you a more exact feel for the distance between the ball and the hole. This means similarly that little mistakes will almost be avoided in lining up the club in the direction of the target (see Diagram 73). If your club is placed in the direction of the target first of all, then it is a simple matter to line up the position of the feet with the target.

When you can combine and mould the two actions of 'taking-up the grip' and 'starting the backswing' into one fluid movement (see Diagram 74), then you will avoid any unnecessary thought processes which might cause you to hesitate. This last point is an important fundamental principle that you must take seriously into consideration. All the aspects which come into play in the battle of mind over matter - body versus mind - can be dispelled ideally by the moulding of the two actions. In the study of movement one speaks of the psychomotor effect. The most important of the psychomotor phenomena, which you will recognize, is the problem that when you are standing at the ball, you have lots of time to think about all the things that you could do wrongly. If in your preparation you have already flipped the switch to actually carry out a good shot, you can fire off your swing in confidence as soon as the fingers of both hands have gripped the club. In this way you can save yourself considerable 'flapping about' with your golf.

If you have the determination, and are consequential in carrying out this procedure prior to each stroke, the problem of a wrong aim will disappear.

150

Diagram 71:
Three paces behind the ball allows for judgement on orientation and distance.

151

Diagram 72:
The aiming procedure starts as one moves towards the ball.

Diagram 73:
The club is lined up with a loose right-handed grip.

Diagram 74:
The grip and the swing are moulded into one movement.

154

Mistakes and Correcting the Swing

Although there is a never-ending palette of swing variations, the typical mistakes that occur are all similar in nature. Experience shows that the cause of a wrong movement is seldom removed. Even when the pro's analysis seems to work better, long term improvement is denied often through the lack of many a golf player's motivation. We believe that the fault of a bad swing lies in an unsuitable (wrong) grip, or similarly a wrong address position.

In order to do justice to the pleasure a golfer has when he achieves good ball impact, we have developed training exercises to cover the most important of the mistakes likely to be made. From these you will be able to correct to the right position and movements gradually. A crash course of changes is thus avoided - we do not believe this to be the correct system anyway. It does no harm at this point to reiterate what we have already said - if you wish seriously to improve yourself, you will not be able to avoid a change of style. Please note that you should restrict yourself to doing this on the driving range. As soon as you are on the golf-course, you should play golf, and not carry on with the training of your techniques.

Take your time with the training exercises and go through them step by step. There is simply no short cut.

BAD BALANCE

To find out if you are changing the centre of your balance enough, stop and hold yourself at the highest point of your backswing (see Diagrams 75 & 76). If, at this point, you are lifting your left foot then your body is moving to the right in order that you do not lose your balance. The more your body moves to the right is an indication that the change in balance was less in the backswing. Only when you do not have to move to the right is this an indication that your balance was very good.

155

Diagram 75:
Bad centre of balance

156

Diagram 76:
Good centre of balance

However this doesn't mean that you HAVE TO place the whole of the weight of your body over the right leg. Better players are able to achieve a greater move of the centre of balance than not such good players. This is because it is easier to keep control when the body moves less to the side. The body's centre of gravity, however, at the end of the backswing should be at least behind the ball. To check this lay a golf-club on your shoulders and hold it down with your hands. If your shoulders have turned through approximately 90 degrees, the club on your shoulders should be pointing to the right of the ball. If you want better proof have a video taken of the movement.

If you ascertain that your change of balance is not enough, then try improving it with this training exercise.

Training Exercise

(On the driving range)
a) Hit ten balls using a reduced swinging action - i.e. a short backswing.
b) Stand again with your legs this time a little further apart than normal and hit another ten balls using a short swing.
c) Repeat another ten shots again with your legs well apart. This time lift your left heel up as you do the backswing.
d) Now do ten shots, and on the backswing lift your left foot for a split second on the backswing - use a half-swing with legs well apart. Make sure that, following the stroke, the whole of your weight is on the left leg.
e) Now do full strokes - use a different club for each stroke and keep lifting your foot as before. Again make sure that at the end of the stroke the whole of your weight is on the left leg.

Carry out the change of balance exercise for two weeks before each time you go out for a round of golf. Take your time over the exercise, but once you are out on the golf-course forget the exercise and put it behind you. In this way your 'feel' and movements will not be disturbed, and your body will gradually learn to adjust to the improved change in balance. After two weeks, carry out the exercise at regular intervals, but at least once a month.

SWINGING FROM THE OUTSIDE TO THE INSIDE

This particular mistake is the most common of all the problems with the swing. The cause lies, also similar to the swing movement 'from the inside to the outside', in the poor coordination of the arms and the body.

The best way to ascertain if you are swinging from the outside to the inside is the divot. It is assumed, however, that you have played the ball off the ground and have taken care to make sure that the sole of the club is flat on the ground. You can check the direction of the path of the club through the ball by carefully laying a club down on the ground along the line and over the middle of the divot. If the divot points to the left or even slightly to the left, then you are swinging from the outside to the inside. If your divot is triangular instead of rectangular and you are not sure what the direction is, then we recommend using a video to ascertain your swing direction. Use the slow motion or frame advance facility on the camera playback as this will be the only way you will be able to detect from which direction the club approaches the ball. Even the experienced pro, by watching your swing, can only guess the direction if he cannot see a clear divot mark.

In order to understand the following exercises you must remember that your arms follow the movement of your shoulders. If your shoulders turn through 90 degrees, your arms will trace also an angle of 90 degrees and no more. So when the arms and upper body are moving in harmony, then they trace out the same angle.

By virtue of the angularity of the wrists, the golf-club will no longer be in a line with the arms - an angle will be formed by the wrists (see Diagram 77). In this position, if you stretched your wrists forward, then the club would again be in line with the left arm (see Diagram 78).

If you push your hands down the club and grip it extremely short (see Diagram 79), you will see whether the arms have moved with the body. This will be the case when the end of the grip comes into contact with the middle of the body somewhere in the region of the belly-button or the sternum. If the arms do not follow the body movement then the coordination between the two is lost.

In such a case the tip of the grip (still pushed up with a short grip) will slip past the body. It will be pure luck that the clubhead will find its way back down to the ball if the arms and body are not moving in unison.

Without this coordination, the energy at the moment of impact will be lost, because the impulse from the arms and body do not complement each other.

This is what happens when you swing from the outside to the inside. The arms are moving faster than the body at the beginning of the backswing. As a result the arms fly somewhat away from the body at the top of the backswing, and on the downswing they take a line farther away from the body than the actual proper line described down to the ball and on to the target.

All the points in the following training exercise, as well as their specific application, will create a movement which will always allow a 'neutral' downswing. To get the full hang of all this we recommend that you try all the exercise points out several times, and as soon as you have dropped to how each of the points feel, select ONE and busy yourself with this until you have reached perfection before you go onto the next.

160

Diagram 77:
The angle - lower arm/club

161

Diagram 78:
Twisting the wrists forward, the club becomes an extension of the left arm.

162

Diagram 79:
Gripping the club extremely short, the tip touches the middle of the body.

163

Take several weeks time for each of the exercises. Observe the golden rule to only do the training on the driving range and then leave them behind when you are out on the golf-course itself. After all you should play golf on the golf-course and you can only do this when you don't have to concentrate on details. Besides, your swing should improve so that when you are in the game, the training automatically flows into it. When carrying out the exercise that follows, take your time and just let the movement 'grow'.

Training Exercise

(On the driving range)
a) Shorten your backswing action (see Diagram 80). Carry out five strokes like this.
b) Rotate your arms and your elbows so that the latter are close together (similar to the volleyball strike position with both arms). The lower arms are also close together (see Diagram 81). Hit 20 balls with your arms in this position - use a short backswing.
c) Now stretch out both of your little fingers, both forefingers and the right thumb (see Diagram 82 & 83). You will recognize this grip from an earlier section in this book. Carry out 20 shots using this grip position.
d) Play 20 balls quite normally. Place a tee in the ground in order to block the swing plane 'from the outside' (see Diagram 84). With this part of the exercise you can check at the same time, how your swing plane has already changed.

Diagram 80:
Short backswing

Diagram 81:
Volleyball arms

166

Diagram 82:
The Ben Hogan-Grip

167

Diagram 83:
The swing using the Ben Hogan-Grip

Diagram 84:
A tee makes you avoid the 'outside swing'.

169

SWINGING FROM THE INSIDE TO THE OUTSIDE

You can also check whether you are swinging from the inside to the outside by analysing your divot. If you are not sure, or you cannot see a distinct divot, then use the aid of a video camera.

Note whether your arms and upper body are moving in unison. This is particularly the case for the first part of the action i.e. when the club is moving away from the ball. The expression used is a "One-Piece-Take-away". In the training exercise which follows we use the abbreviation OPT to describe this movement.

In swing movements, which are spoken of as 'from the inside to the outside', the club usually starts from the outside on the backswing. This results in a sharp movement to the inside as the club moves through the ball. As in the swing 'from the outside to the inside' the club reacts to the movements in the backswing.

Dependent on the size of the player, the more the club moves away from the correct path as it follows through the ball position, the less the extent of the slice. It will make hardly any difference whether it is from the outside - in or from the inside - out.

The direction of the club as it passes through the ball is largely dependent on the first inch or two of the backswing movement. If the swing plane is steep (see Part 1), the club will move less to the inside on the Takeaway. Similarly, if the swing plane is flatter, the club will move much more to the inside on the Takeaway.

Basically, the initial movement of the club determines the direction of the aim by itself, if you are using the correct address position. Adopt the correct address position, and then turn your shoulders away from the target for an OPT and let your arms (and the club) go to the inside to exactly the right degree. First of all check your address position. If you are standing well and your grip is OK, then the following training exercise will help you to bring your swing onto the right lines.

Training Exercise

(On the driving range)

a) Stand at the ball and pull back your club about five degrees by turning your shoulders. Do this by keeping your arms and shoulders stiff i.e. without using your wrists (see Diagram 85).

b) Now turn your shoulders to a ten degree position without using your wrists (see Diagram 85).

c) Now this time turn your shoulders 20 degrees (see also Diagram 85).

d) Bring your wrists now into play matching the turn of your shoulders. First of all to five degrees OPT and then angle the club (see Diagram 86).

e) Do the same but this time turning the shoulders and angling the club to ten degrees (see Diagram 86).

f) Turn again now with an angle of 20 degrees OPT (see Diagram 86).

g) Repeat points (d) to (f) and hit the ball at the same time.

171

Diagram 85:
The One-Piece-Takeaway: shoulders, arms, grip and clubhead move in unison.

172

Diagram 86:
Angular timing: very early, early and normal angularity produces a straight swing.

LOOSE JOINTS

In order to create energy for the swing it is necessary to produce a certain tension in the muscles of particular parts of the body. If your address position and grip are correct this will happen almost automatically. However there are two assumptions regarding the tension and whether it is maintained: You must not change the angle of the bend of your right knee or your left elbow at all as you do your backswing. Both of these joints must be kept at the same angle. If you let one of these joints slacken, for example increase the angle of the bend, then this would lengthen the muscles brought into play. A muscle that has been lengthened loses its strength. In part, the stresses in the ligaments will be transmitted into the bones. All this potential will be lost the moment that your joints give way.

The principles of the build up of tension for the golf swing look like this:

Your right foot is just about at right-angles to the target on the ground. Your shoes have been fitted with spikes. In the backswing, your hips turn to the right and it will be the spikes which prevent your right foot from turning. If you are not wearing spikes it will be the force of gravity of your body which holds the position of the foot on the ground. Since you do not change the angle of the right knee, the muscles and ligaments keep the tension. The hips turn against the fixed position of the foot and spikes. Thus you now have tension from the feet up to the hips (see Diagram 87).

The shoulders can be turned further than the hips. Therefore tension doesn't end at the hips. On the contrary it runs further up over the diagonal stomach muscles and along the large back muscles into the shoulders (see Diagram 88).

From the shoulders it continues down the arm and through the tensioned left elbow into the hands (see Diagram 89). The wrists must be able to withstand the pressure produced.

174

Diagram 87:
One can see from the creases in the clothes just how much tension there is from the feet to the hips ...

175

Diagram 88:
... and the tension from the hips to the shoulders.

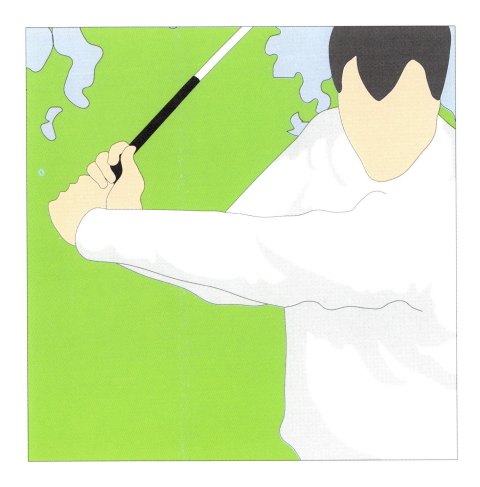

Diagram 89:
The tension runs further - from the shoulders over the arms into the hands ...

177

Diagram 90:
... and onto the clubhead.

178

Diagram 91:
This is the run of the tension through the body (and the golf-club).

179

The tension eventually continues on into the golf-club itself. You can see that the shaft bends when the body changes direction (see Diagram 90).

An analysis of the whole movement shows that there is a tension chain reaction running from the spikes right through into the clubhead (see Diagram 91).

Many golfers do not realize that it is the tension in the muscles which builds up the energy and which is fired off at the moment of impact with the ball. If your backswing is exaggerated, energy is lost, because when the joints break from the correct position the tension in the muscles collapses. If one carefully examines the anatomical processes involved, you will find, as mentioned above, that it is not the muscles alone which come into play in the build-up of tension, but also the structural and skeletal positioning of the joints. For example, in the case of the knee joint, there are stress-forces which stretch the ligaments and the harder parts of the meniscus. Both contribute to the building up of tension. Please note that by using the word tension, this should not be confused with cramp, which is the opposite.

In the following diagrams you will see loose (i.e. wrong) joint positions (Diagrams 92-95). You will perhaps recognize one or two golf swing styles from your circle of acquaintances!

TIP Step by step, go through in your mind the points listed above regarding the build up of tension from the spikes to the clubhead. You will find where you will be able to improve your backswing stroke. Soon you will be able to sense how to create the optimum tension in your muscles, and you will be surprised just how little your backswing needs to be. In this way you will be able to have your first practical experience in golf, namely understanding what is meant by the expression "less is more".

Diagram 92:
Tension too loose at the knee

Diagram 93:
Tension in the left elbow too loose

Diagram 94:

Tension too loose in the shoulders

184

Diagram 95:
Tension in the left wrist too loose

185

MOVEMENT OF THE BODY'S CENTRE OF BALANCE

Centre of Balance - Horizontal

There are some theories concerning the swing which encourage a considerable horizontal movement of the body, and there are others which don't. The real value of such a movement is that the body mass will be swung into the stroke as it is made. Actually there is already a suitable measure of change in the centre of balance during a normal turn of the shoulders. How one achieves this has already been covered earlier (see Diagrams 75 & 76).

You can move your upper body somewhat harder to the right and thus create more power. However this will only function to a certain degree, above which you tend to lose control of the swing. The assumption is always that you don't let your joints give.

Better players are able to increase their horizontal movement. A study in the USA has confirmed this for both amateur and pros (during the US Tour and US Senior Tour tournaments). However be careful, because it means, on the other hand, that you will have more control over your swing if you do not over-exaggerate the sideways movement.

Centre of Balance - Vertical

While there are various theories and recommendations regarding the horizontal movement of the centre of balance, and how much this should be done (-we have produced a suitable compromise above), the opinion of the professional school of thought is unanimously agreed regarding the vertical change of the centre of balance - the centre of balance of the body should remain at the same height during the movement. This is, however, only valid for the backswing and follow through just before and immediately after the moment of impact with the ball. What happens in the follow through well after impact is relatively unimportant. *The best check of whether the swing is smooth is to observe the movement of the head.*

Pros have gradually given up the habit of gripping the pupil by the hair in order to restrain the movement, as this tends to hamper the

186

freedom of movement in the turn of the body for the stroke. For some players this method of fixating the head, prevents the change of balance onto the left leg altogether.

Equally, we recommend you do not use this method, but advise earnestly that you lay a great deal of worth on keeping the head still, at least during the first part of the swing action i.e. from the moment of the backswing up until the moment of impact.

> **TIP** Sometimes it is a good idea to practice in front of a mirror. Simulate a swing without the ball and observe your head and whether it bobs up and down or stays still. If you are not sure use a video camera to assist.

If you notice that you are "ducking", first of all check whether you are bending your knees during the movement. If this is the case, stand as upright as you can (without locking your knees back) and build this into your pre-shot routine. Check also your address position with regard to the ski-jump example earlier (see Diagram 68).

A vertical movement is not caused necessarily by a grip or address position problem, contrary to most of the other problems. The body has to learn to maintain the upright position during the movement. To a certain extent it will cost energy to keep the tip of the nose at the same height during the swing action. If you have found you have a vertical movement, and there is no fault with your knees giving, then the following training exercise will assist.

187

Training Exercise

a) Pick up a 7-iron. Pick a target on the ground about 30 yards in front of you. On tiptoe (i.e. you are now taller), try to hit ten balls one after the other.

b) Now bend your knees so that you are shorter, and so that you can balance yourself better. Play ten balls into the same 30-yard target area.

c) Do a three-quarter swing (80-120 yards) with 15 balls.

d) Stand with your feet well apart (broad address position) (again on your tiptoes). Emphasize your centre of balance, but still hold the tip of your nose at the same height, and hit 25 balls. Have a friend check you out.

The effort you have to use in standing on the tips of your toes while keeping the tip of your nose at the same height, will give you the feel of how exhausting it is to do this. Simultaneously you will be able to level out the differences in height which occur in the swing more easily. All this will give you a feeling for what the meaning of a vertical movement is in practice, and allow you to control it better. At the end of the training exercise you will hardly tend to "duck" any more. Repeat the exercise two or three times on the driving range but leave the technique behind when you are on the golf-course.

TIMING

Besides both the large impulses created by the turn of the shoulders and the change of centre of balance, there are several other impulses employed which increase the energy to be used.

Just visualise a shot-putter, who before he moves forward, stretches down with the shot nestling hard into his neck. Anyone who has ever held one of these shots will know how heavy it is (for women almost 6 kgs and for men almost 8 kgs). With his large torso muscles, and at the same time spinning round as fast as he can, the athlete lifts the shot up.

When the shot (still held hard into the neck) has reached a certain speed, he begins to use the (smaller) arm muscles and then the (even smaller) finger muscles. If he were to do all this in the opposite order of priority he would hardly begin to move the shot.

How much energy is developed depends on the decisive moment at which each of the muscle groups are progressively brought into action.

Just as in the shot-put, in golf there is an optimum timing for each of the parts of the impulses used. The better these impulses complement each other, both in time and space, means that more energy will be built up. This is the secret of stroke distance as well as accuracy, which, unlike the shot-put, is also required in golf. This is why so many unathletic players can reach such enormous distances. Ian Woosnam, a top world class smally-built player belonging to the true "long hitters", achieves his power by combining the individual impulses in a particularly good way.

For the player himself this is all contained in one movement - he doesn't think of the various impulses, but rather feels a progressive chain reaction in the flow of the impulses - simply ONE single action. World class players can hit the ball particularly far because of their technique. If you have exceptionally tall and well built muscular players, then one sees absolutely tremendous long drives being produced. Examples of this are the US Pros Fred Couples, Davis Love and of course Tiger Woods.

Some differently talented people manage to put all the part-movements into one in a number of ways. In the science of movement one also speaks of "coupling ability".

When you try to carry out a complicated movement, it will always depend on the circumstances. If you are relaxed and 'up to the mark' then success in executing a good golf stroke will come on its own. Sometimes the timing will last for a round or two. If cramp or stress factors creep in, the same movement will become more or less robotic.

How you can influence this was covered in the chapter concerning "Your form on the day" in Part 1. You can improve your timing for a golf tournament, or simply just for a good day's golf, by trying the following training exercise. You should repeat the exercise every now and again.

Besides having a correct address position (only achievable by using a neutral grip), we believe that timing represents a further important factor in making a successful golfer. You can only develop and maintain good timing if you have learned to be aware of the clubhead and know the 'feel' of it. As you will have gathered long ago reading this book, many of the training exercises are all about assimilating the 'feel' of the swing in golf. In the following training exercise about timing, we have divided it into two parts. In the first part you will find out how to regain your timing if you have lost it temporarily. The second part is for all those, who have a long-term problem with their timing.

Training Exercise

Timing - Part 1

a) First of all do some warming-up exercises - as depicted in the section „Golf gymnastics" later in this part of Straight Golf.

b) Hit five balls with a normal swing speed using a medium-iron.

c) Now increase the speed of your swing - stroke by stroke.

d) When you have reached the maximum tempo, reduce it, stroke by stroke. (When doing this avoid putting a brake on the club.)

e) Now change the club you are using, and the speed of the swing after every stroke. For example take a 5-iron and carry out a fast swing. Then take a driver and use a slow swing.

Timing - Part 2

a) Borrow a few clubs (men's and ladies') of various makes and style and change over to a different club after each shot.

b) Shut your eyes and change your timing. Make a note in your mind of the varying differences in the weight of the clubheads, so that you can be aware of which speed you were most at home with.

c) Buy yourself a special club which has a particularly whippy shaft (and is correspondingly thin). With this, your swing must be carried out with care, otherwise it will literally wrap itself round your neck. Where can you obtain one of these training aids? Any good pro will be able to help you!

d) Increase your grip at every shot until you cannot grip any firmer. Loosen the grip of your hands gradually at each successive stroke until you are just able to hold it safely. Note the weight of the clubhead.

If you wish to work more intensively on the swing speed then you should take time for a few weeks or even months to gradually work your way through the exercise above. For anybody who has a really serious timing problem, then besides the long-term work, you should go through the thought process prior to any day of golf. You should carry out at least one of the exercises from Part 1 on the driving range before a round of golf. In your pre-shot routine, watch out all the time that you are holding the club LOOSELY in the right hand. This ensures you can still keep the feel of its weight in your mind.

Mistakes and Correcting Your Short Game

First of all you must note several basic ground rules. Once you have mastered the ground rules, then you can go on to the rest of the points.

Ground rule No 1: *Play the ball as flat as you possibly can!*

Play the ball as flat as the situation will allow. A flat ball is easier to hit. Contrary to a full stroke you only need to sway your body weight to the left and not use your wrists.

If the ball is lying on flat ground, it will hardly be possible to play an accurate shot. In most cases you will slice the ball or hit the ground before the ball. Play this shot from the right foot, bring the weight to the left and keep the hands firm. In this way contact with the ball will be a surety. Even if you don't hit the ball cleanly, the miss-shot will not end up too far from where it would have with a good shot. If you try to play the ball up, a mis-shot will have a fairly catastrophic effect.

Ground rule No 2: *Accelerate the club through the ball!*

Even for short play, accelerate the club through the ball. A club which has a constant 'through-speed' or is even slowing down, will always be unstable. If you do not hit the ball cleanly or hit the ground before the ball, the striking face of the club will twist easily and there will be a mis-shot. On the other hand, a club which is accelerating, is considerably more stable, and will have quite a positive effect despite a less than perfect shot or a shot out of the rough.

193

Ground rule No 3: *Look at both points of impact!*

Look at the lie of your ball and decide how you will play it. Decide which PART OF THE STRIKING FACE you will hit the ball with. Now decide which POINT ON THE BALL you will strike with the clubface. Don't lose sight of the two points you have identified in your pre-shot routine. Switch your eyes backwards and forwards between the two points of impact. Just prior to playing the ball, and only then, keep your eyes trained on the ball.

POOR LENGTH WHEN PUTTING

From Part 1, you will know that the putting action is a pendulum swing movement. Make sure, when you are performing this shot, that the head of the putter moves to each side of the centre point by equal amounts. This is only possible when the putter is swung from the shoulders unhindered. This will be easiest for you if you use a grip in which the left wrist is fixed (see Diagram 96). Of course you can switch between all the other grip techniques. We recommend, however, the Bernhard Langer-Grip as this avoids the problem of the left wrist giving way. Simply the effect of the fixed left wrist improves the accuracy of your aim, and with it the accuracy of distance. For a long putt the cause of poor accuracy in the length is to do exclusively with bad ball impact.

If you wish to improve the accuracy of length for medium and short putts, take some time to practice the following exercise on the practice green.

By using this training exercise you will be able to learn how to move the putter freely and swing it like a pendulum. The characteristic of the pendulum movement is that it oscillates to either side by equal amounts at a precise and constant speed.

Training Exercise

Before you begin ask your pro to lend you a set of weighing scales for golf-clubs.

a) On the training green lay down two golf-clubs in line with the grips butting onto each other.

b) Put the head of your putter down on the ground where the two ends of the grips meet.

c) Now swing your club like a pendulum the same distance to each side (see Diagrams 97 & 98). With your eyes check how much to each side the club is swung - the length of the grip sections of the two clubs on the ground will aid you in this.

d) Continue swinging the putter until you can gauge in your mind whether it is heavier or lighter than your pitching wedge.

e) Pick up your pitching wedge and do the same as you did with the putter. Was your estimate correct?

f) Measure the weight of both of these clubs - if your pro hasn't got a set of scales then a pair of household scales will suffice. Repeat the exercise at (d) and (e) above to check the measurements. Practice this for as long as it takes for you to really recognize a difference.

The important thing is for you to be able to get into your mind a certain 'freedom of the putting head'. Your brain will only learn what sort of distance you reach, with each particular pull back in the pendulum movement, when you swing through by the same amount. If you were to apply a brake or force the movements of the pendulum action, initially you would get the ball closer up to the hole, but you would not gain experience of judging that you come FREELY and properly to the end of the swing in proportion to the pull back.

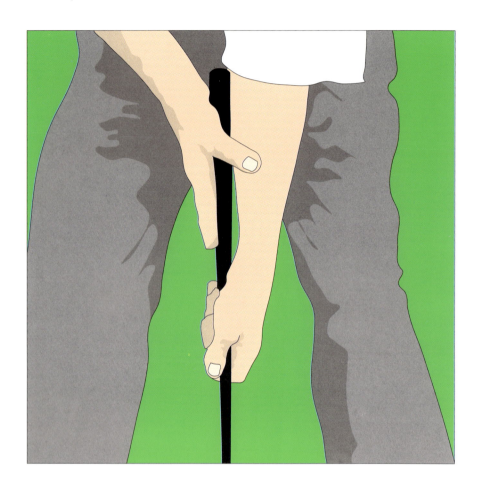

Diagram 96:
The Bernhard Langer-Grip

Diagram 97:
A pendulum moves to each side ...

Diagram 98:
... to the same amount.

198

The following example illustrates this phenomenon:

Place yourself about 15 feet away from a hole. Your 'feel' for the ball will automatically adapt the amount of the distance to pull back your club. Possibly your 'feel' will tell you once you have pulled your club back - "Now if I follow through the same amount that I have done on the backswing, the ball will go too far!" Despite this, in such a situation, you must carry on with the stroke. It is important that you do not try to influence (or brake) the pendulum motion of your putter. You must play a relaxed stroke. It is the brain which gradually adapts itself to the right amount needed. Just simply let the ball roll on too far. When you actually see the result, your brain will adapt and adjust for the right amount of pendulum required for the next stroke. Consequently, after nine holes on the training green, your 'touch' will begin to improve, and your judgement and stroke will adapt itself to each distance you meet.

If you adopt a style of relaxed putting, the pressure you meet on the green will turn into pleasure in carrying out the movement. Imagine the strength you will get, even in the most difficult situations, once you know your putt is executed in a relaxed manner.

POOR AIM WHEN PUTTING

By swinging the club correctly like a pendulum you can hit the ball better and thus also achieve a better aim when putting. Nevertheless it can happen that, despite a good pendulum swing, you are not able to get rid of an aiming problem. In this case, first of all, you must check your stance. Lay a club down exactly in the direction of your play and check your stance as well as the line of your hips and shoulders. If these are all correct, then in order of priority check the following:

- Are your eyes directly over the ball? (See the method with the mirror in Part 1.)
- Are you carrying out your pre-shot routine of at least three paces behind the ball?
- Use of a putter grip which is flattened off (on the thumb side in order to assist with the aiming (see Diagram 99)?
- Is your right wrist staying in the same position?
- Take a video recording to see if all is correct.

199

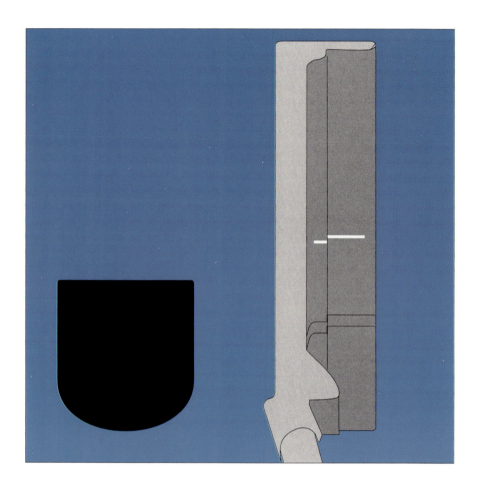

Diagram 99:

On the left is the cross section of flat sided putter grip, which assists in aiming. If the flat side is facing forwards then the front of the clubface is aimed correctly.

Diagram 100:
Bunker shot without a follow through

BUNKER SHOT - WITHOUT A FOLLOW THROUGH

The shot which is probably the most common is the bunker shot without a follow through being played i.e. the club does not swing through and out of the sand (see Diagram 100).

Imagine you are skimming a flat stone across a pond. The moment that the stone looses its energy, it sinks into the water.

Just as the flight of the stone hangs in the water, so does your sand iron 'hang' in the bunker if the swing is not followed through. In Part 1 we described a number of ways of avoiding a ricochet. The sandwedge will work better if:

 ... you open the clubface;
 ... you accelerate the club;
 ... you swing from the outside to the inside;
 ... you 'burst out' less sand.

When the sand is softer and deeper, you will have to combine some of these factors to get the best result. How you do this will be up to you. The most important thing is that you must develop a 'feel' for yourself on how you move the club through the sand and achieve a follow through (see Diagram 101).

In the following training exercise note that, above all, you must swing the club on the follow through to the end i.e. over your left shoulder, irrespective whether your stroke is a long or a short one (see Diagram 102).

Training Exercise

a) Hit five balls out of the bunker with an open clubface.
b) Keep the clubface open. For the next five balls accelerate your stroke.
c) With the clubface still open, accelerate the club yet faster. For the next five balls swing from the outside to the inside.
d) Repeat what you have done in steps (a) to (c). With the next five shots don't scoop up as much sand as before.

BUNKER SHOT - TRAJECTORY TOO FLAT

If you play the ball too flat out of the bunker, you will be confronted, some time or other, with the problem that the high bunker lip will block your shot. The question is, how does one get the ball to curve up high out of the bunker?

For this shot you have to violate one of the basic ground rules of golf - as an exception. In order to achieve a high trajectory you require more loft at the moment of impact than your sand iron normally allows. Carry out this exercise:

Training Exercise

a) Slightly open the clubface.
b) Aim to the left of the target.
c) Now carry out ten bunker shots using only the arms and a lot of hand and wrist movement.
d) Next, do some normal bunker shots. Swing in such a manner so that you can actually see the clubface as it emerges out of the sand (see Diagram 103). As a result, the ball will have a high trajectory.

203

Diagram 101:
Bunker shot with follow through

Diagram 102:
Bunker shot with follow through over the left shoulder

Diagram 103:
If your hands 'spoon' up the sand under the ball you can see the clubface.

Smart Shots

PLUGGED BALL - IN A BUNKER (1)

If your ball is trapped (i.e. 'submerged' in the sand - golfers use the expression "plugged"), first of all consider whether it is at all playable. If you can see the ball quite clearly and the lip of the bunker is quite flat, and the sand soft and loose, then the decision is relatively easy - you can play the ball. In all other cases you must rely on your own experience whether you can get the ball out or not. You must also develop a sense of when you are going to declare the ball as unplayable. Once you realize your limitations in this respect, be consistent about your decisions. Sometimes, nevertheless, you will get the feeling that, despite a seemingly impossible situation you could still be able to play the ball. We believe that when you are in such a situation, occasionally you should at least attempt a shot - even at the risk of a 'fluff shot' with the result that the ball does not come out of the bunker.

Training Exercise

a) Step into the bunker and put your foot down on the ball in order to plug it. Take your SW and close the face a little (see Diagram 104). Stand so that you are aiming to the left.

b) Even if your club meets a lot of resistance in the sand, try above all to complete the follow through. Shorten the backswing and increase the follow through movement towards the target.

c) Try this out with varying positions of the clubhead e.g. sometimes close the clubface more, sometimes less.

d) Now do the same exercise with your PW. Note how high and fast the ball now moves off to the right.

Diagram 104:
With a plugged ball close the clubface.

208

With this last exercise you can train for the case of having a plugged ball in the sand bunker.

To get out of the bunker, you will soon learn what is the best angle of attack to hold the clubface . You should also note which sand consistency allows you to make best use of the pitching wedge. Eventually you may well decide that it is best to use the pitching wedge anyway for this shot - just as most of the pros do.

PLUGGED BALL - IN A BUNKER (2)

If the lip of the bunker is in the way and the flag is not too far off, there is yet another way to be able to play the ball. Beware though - this shot is extremely difficult. It is possibly the most difficult shot of all. However, it is possible to learn how to execute it. We want to teach you a few special tricks anyway! Try it out - you will need to use a putter.

Training Exercise

a) Go onto the putting green and practice some putts (about 2 yards) using the tip end of the putter until you are able to hit the ball consistently. You must make sure, as you address the ball, that you switch your eyes from putter to ball and fix the point of impact you will use.

b) Now go into the practice bunker and play some plugged balls out of the sand in the same way. The main difference is the dynamics - you must 'putt' much harder.

c) For this you must be able to see the rear half of the ball. Note the shape of the tip of your putter and hold it so that it will achieve the optimum effect (see Diagram 105 & 106).

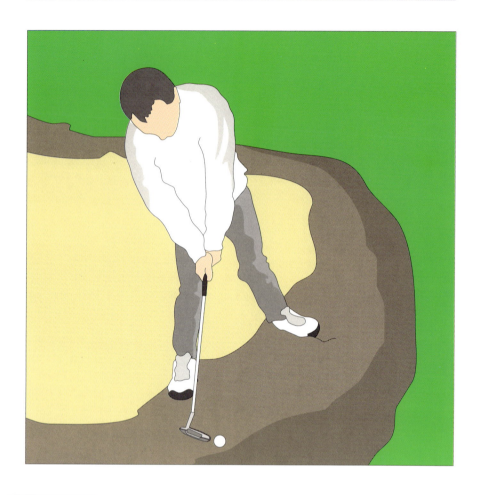

Diagram 105:
Hold the tip of the putter exactly behind the ball ...

Diagram 106:
... and fix your gaze on the rear half of the ball.

HALF-PLUGGED BALL IN A FAIRWAY BUNKER

This situation is relatively common (see Diagram 107). Do not expect too much. Because of the bad lie, the ball cannot be simply swept away (as we explained in Part 1 in the chapter on "Difficult Situations") - and the shot length will be considerably reduced. If the lip of the bunker is really low and flat you can use a particular technique, which will manage to achieve some reasonable distance, in comparison to other bunker shots one is sometimes forced to play, and which give practically no shot length at all.

Training Exercise

a) Take two to three irons more than you would normally use. Think about a shot that is going to have a low trajectory and will roll out a long way.
b) Play the ball from a position opposite the middle of your feet. Grip somewhat shorter than normal and take up a good address position.
c) Open the clubface quite wide. Accordingly, aim to the left because the ball is going to move off to the right.
d) Use a three-quarter swing and strike the ball just underneath the middle of its girth irrespective of whether you will impact at this point with the sand or the ball itself first. Concentrate your eyes hard on the point of impact of the ball.

A BALL LYING JUST AT THE MOWN EDGE OF THE GREEN

If the ball is lying in such a position, then the resistance created by the grass is so great that you will hardly be able to estimate the stroke length. The tip of your putter will help you out here also, as it will glide through the thickest of grass with practically no resistance at all (see Diagram 108).

212

Diagram 107:
The lightly plugged, long bunker shot

213

The training exercise for this shot is the same as the first part of the one given earlier in "Plugged ball - in a bunker (2)". After you have putted a few balls on the green with the tip of the putter, play some shots like this from the grass strip bordering the green in order to get the 'feel' of the speed of the ball. You will be surprised how easily the head of the putter cuts through the grass.

A BALL LYING UP AGAINST A HEDGE OR FENCE, WALL OR ON THE COURSE BOUNDARY

For this shot you only need to close the clubface and strike the ball normally (see Diagram 109). Additionally play the ball a little farther from the right foot. Make a compensation for the ball which will veer off to the left. Note: The ball will have a very flat trajectory and will roll on - use a club one to three numbers less than normal, dependent on how much you close the clubface.

BALL IN THE DEEP ROUGH AT A SHORT DISTANCE FROM THE FLAG

This stroke has been seldom necessary over the last few decades, even on British coastal courses. On the other hand, throughout the American tournament courses since the 70's and 80's, particularly the US-Open ones, it was often necessary. In the meanwhile there are several courses in Germany which have followed this fashion, and one finds quite heavy roughs in the immediate vicinity of the green.

If your ball is lying in the rough in such a situation, and it is only a short distance to the flag, a really heavy club (SW) will help you enormously. If your home course has some of these types of rough you should buy yourself the heaviest possible sandwedge club you can find. If you have any doubts, ask your pro if he can make your club heavier.

This shot is all about being able to swing the club slowly and despite this not get caught up in the rough.

214

Diagram 108:
The tip of the putter cuts easily through the thickest grass.

215

Diagram 109:
Using a normal address position open the clubface hard.

216

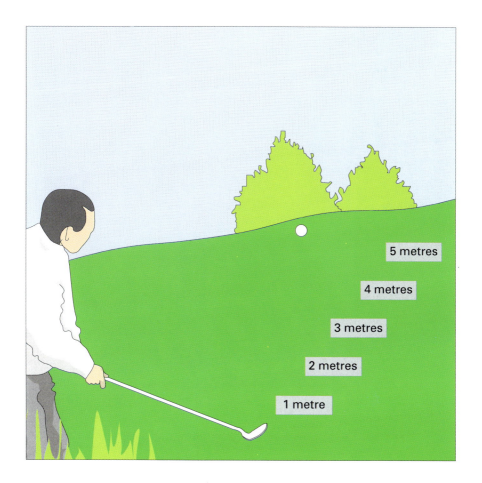

Diagram 110:
The best way to practice shots out of the roughs by the green is over short distances.

Training Exercise

a) Open your sandwedge a little. Grip a little firmer than normal. Bring your body weight more over the left leg.

b) Play the shot expressly using your wrists. Let the club swing freely on the follow through without holding back and accelerate as fast as you can.

c) First of all aim to play the ball for only a short distance out of the rough. One after the other, aim to play five shots in turn to a distance of 1,2,3,4, and 5 yards (see Diagram 110).

With this shot the ball will have no spin and so it will roll far. The higher you can play the ball the quicker it will come to a stop. Impact with the ball is more important in this shot than the height of the trajectory. In such a situation, take heart and play the ball a little too far rather than getting stuck in the rough.

THE BALL LYING IN A DIVOT

If the ball is lying in a divot, you must first of all decide whether you can play it all. You can usually sensibly make a shot if at least half of the ball is protruding above the surface of the grass. In such a case, play the ball well from the right almost opposite your right foot. Use an iron one to two numbers more than normal. So instead of a number 5-iron use a 6 or a 7.

THE BALL IS TRAPPED AGAINST A FALLEN TREE BRANCH

This shot can be really dangerous and will often end up in disaster. Think carefully if you really want to play the shot if the ball is lying in direct contact with a branch lying on the ground. We recommend that in cases of branches having a diameter greater than your little finger, play safe and declare the ball as unplayable - alternatively you could try a short chip. You should only risk a shot if the larger branches or twigs are particularly dry and brittle.

For this shot play the ball well off to the right foot. Shorten your swing and angle your wrists only a little. Use your body weight in order to emphasize the follow through against the resistance.

Strategy

During our work on „Straight Golf", as we made the German television film and wrote this book, we were surprised at just how many different components there were which had an influence on the playing strength of the golfer, and which were totally neglected because the art of technique always took the upper hand. Factors such as fitness and condition, mental approach, strategy and equipment are barely recognized and discussed in normal golf training. Since we are trying to go through all these subjects (using a golfing backdrop), as optimally as possible, here are a number of playing strategies for you. Try them out, and discover which ones suit your temperament. Sometimes it is worthwhile combining the one or other of the points together. It is important to hit on a particular thread of strategy which will help you keep your game up, as well as safe, and which you should use, not only at the beginning of each season, but prior to each round and each stroke you play.

KEEPING THE BALL IN PLAY

Make it a top priority to keep the ball in play. Very often this means shorter distances, sometimes chosen intentionally to match the situation, and which otherwise, by choosing a different route, would only have less effect. It is also often sufficient to pick out the broadest and easiest place where your ball should land. Check out whether, even with one of your worst or typical miss-shots, you can also reach these spots on the course, and still end up with a playable shot. If you want to play a safe game, note the following points:

> **TIP** Aim at the broadest point of the fairway and select a suitable club for the shot. Aim for the centre of the green. Lay up from the course hazards. If in doubt ensure you drop your shot in front of the hazard. However, if you are intent on landing on the green, always choose a club a number less than you think you need (e.g. instead of a 6-iron use a 5). If your ball is lying in a thicket or in a deep rough, chose the safest and most direct route back onto the fairway.

221

FEEDBACK METHOD OF IMPROVEMENT

Using 'feedback' is the best way to learn. If you learn to use your senses to give you feedback about your movements, you will be able to improve much quicker, and reach a considerably higher level sooner in your golf. This is equally valid for all golf strokes, whether it be a drive or a putt on the green.

Training Exercise

a) Don't judge your strokes on ball impact and result (ball trajectory) alone. Consider what your body does as well.

b) Check and observe with your watch just how long 20 seconds is.

c) Hold the end position of your follow through for 20 seconds. 'Soak up' the feeling (see Diagram 111).

d) Ask yourself the following questions:
- Where was the weight of my body?
- Was I standing relaxed?
- Was my balance correct?
- Were any of my muscles strained?
- Where did the club end up?
- Am I gripping the same as in my address position?
- Is the ball trajectory as good as my body feels it was?
- Was the impact with the ball as good as my body feels it was?

e) If you can get this information, it shouldn't be difficult for you to compare it with your training.

f) Work out now what you have to change for the next stroke. In this manner you should continually develop your swing, not only on the driving range but also during a tournament.

Diagram 111:
After the swing - time to soak up the feeling.

223

CONTROL

Imagine you are a skier! Do you follow the skis, or do the skis follow you?

Which is the most successful attitude for you to be in, so that you are able to maintain control of all the various situations during a round of golf?

In order to ensure that it is not the skis which are showing you the way, but that you are the one who is determining the way forward, first of all you must work up your pre-shot routine. The more exact you are able to carry this out, each and every time, means that you will be better equipped to keep and retain control on the golf-course.

We do not mean that by using this strategy you should always choose the easiest and safest approach - on the contrary, it serves to teach you to control yourself and your body movements. This means not only your physical actions but also your mental thoughts.

Possibly in the next few years you will hit many a ball into the water, out of bounds, near to the flag or even get a hole-in-one! All this will be a surety. Even a world class player knows that, in the next few tournaments he plays, he will sometimes have super shots and sometimes absolutely terrible ones. If this is known beforehand why should one get so emotional about it all? If you ever get into this frame of mind, just be clear that it was pre-destined anyway! Just remember - it could turn out the other way round. In this way it will allow you to concentrate more and get the best out of yourself in situations like these. So why lose control?

We recommend that, with the exception of the hole-in-one, which really calls for a celebration, you should be prepared for anything and not over-react too much to events, so that your self-control and ball control stays at a pitch. So the next time you hit the ball into the water, don't be upset. It was going to happen sometime anyway! Just concentrate on the next stroke you have to play. This strategy will pay off at the end of the round.

Also, when perhaps now and again, you succeed in hitting the ball very close to the flag, just stay calm. Celebrate perhaps that evening after the round - well just a little! Staying calm about such things will allow you to stay up to the mark and not concern yourself with emotional reactions. In the long run you will hole a few birdie putts. Just take a look at some of the golfers around you. Most of them are slaves to their emotions, not only on the golf-course but also on the driving range and even in the club-house later. Try to lift yourself above all this. Just have a little smile to yourself about it. You will know that things just happen from time to time. Simple joy and pleasure is always more beautiful and lasts longer than over-exaggerated jubilation.

There is a direct connection between the last two strategies mentioned. It is exactly at the moment in time that one can motorically learn the most, namely when one has completed the swing (feedback method), that the emotional information begins to flood in and gives the data required to be able to improve for the next shot (control).

> **TIP** Maintain full control of your emotions, so that your brain is left open for the learning process! Carry on with the same routine, irrespective of whether the last shot was good or bad. Maintain your rhythm. In certain particular situations don't speed up - or slow down either!

"GETTING INTO THE GAME"

Before each tournament round, do everything you can to 'get' into the game. For this you will need peace and quiet. Even if you don't have as much time as you would wish, your inner calm must be undisturbed. Build yourself up. Start the round with a good ball impact. Don't try in particular to make long drives. A good first stroke with a 5-iron will give more self-confidence than a long drive. This will pay off in the long run at the end of the round, because the self confidence that you build up during the round is the best sort of all. Even if you have to swallow a couple of poor holes at the beginning of a round, the score will often be better at the end because your self-confidence will lead to many more good holes being played than poor ones if you are continually always holding yourself back.

Use this principle fairly flexibly. Be creative! You can count yourself as being 'into the game', during the season even if you aren't worried about the result, and have used it simply to build up your swing.

Similarly, 'getting into the game' can also mean that your strategy is to play for "a systematically planned series of successes" rather than a win. In order to achieve this aim, you must be prepared always to play a little less offensively which, of course, can lead to you being temporarily a stroke or two down.

Again, you can adopt a strategy that on a single hole, on the way from the tee-off to the green, you 'get into the game', so to speak, by teeing-off with 5-wood rather than a driver. This will mean that you give up distance, but build up on good ball impact instead. Play onto the green with a smoothly swung 5-iron instead of a 'hectic' 7-iron. Aim for the centre of the green. Your self-confidence will have been bolstered up by both of these good impacts, so that it is possibly not only sure you will achieve a PAR, but maybe even a birdie with the putt.

PATIENCE ON THE GOLF-COURSE

Practice keeping your patience! Even if it is difficult for you, force yourself to do things slowly and always with the same action. Keep your rhythm. Don't speed up during the round. On the way to the golf-course, drive your car in a relaxed manner. Take your time quietly to get together all the necessities (balls, tees, refreshments for the round etc.)

Irrespective of how you do your warming-up exercises and how many practice shots you do, seek pleasure with every single movement and look

226

for a quiet spot on your own, where you can concentrate on your body movements and clubhead. If people speak to you often, just smile and don't chat back a lot.

Go out in a frame of mind that you are going to tee-off with a good impact, regardless of whether you have to take a 5-wood or even a 7-iron to start. Just enjoy the feeling when you note in the middle of a round that you are well up to the mark. Always keep within your limitations. Keep your play within these limits and try to stay at this level - i.e., don't strain to play absolutely super shots all the time. Save yourself for when the situation really demands them.

'ATTACKING' THE FLAG

While you are still quite some way away from the hole, play conservatively. When you have a chance to play the ball close onto the flag with a chipping wedge, ready to birdie out, THEN play more on the offensive. Everything that is anywhere in the area of the green (short pitch, lob, chip), you should really try to hole out. Your play should become more aggressive the closer you come to the flag. There are 'red' areas for every strength of player, and in these one must play for safety. However, as soon as you are in a 'green' area, then you should open up your game and try to hole out or drop the ball dead (see Diagram 112).

Despite being close up to the flag, a risky shot should be an exception, such as where there could be a danger that it will drop into water or out of bounds. Here you should choose the safest playing route dependent on the situation. When you are putting, each ball should have a 'fighting' chance, or at least the momentum, to reach the hole.

A particularly long drive should have a fighting chance to finish up as a birdie after several further strokes. Similarly, as a general rule, a good shot with an iron is still so far off from the flag that the probability is, the putt following it up, will slip past the hole rather than into it.

227

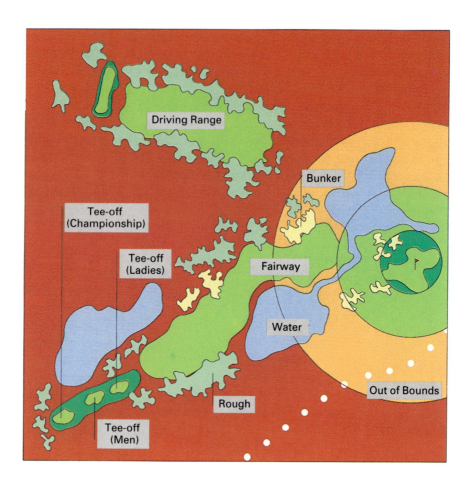

Diagram 112:
Don't attack until you are in the green shaded area!

228

There is a 50% possibility of holing out with a putt if the previous shot was played as a successful SHORT iron stroke. From this distance one should attack. Even if the stroke is played 'perfectly', it will be clear to all, that this shot will seldom go straight into the hole.

Most of the time only really perfectly executed putts and chips, carried out in the vicinity of the green, will hole out often. You should always try your best.

Naturally there will be occasions when you should play defensively in the green area near the flag e.g., when there is a little water hazard between the ball and the flag. In this case you will have to decide for yourself where the dividing line is between the 'red' and the 'green' area.

Short play is of immense importance for a good score. This is the sphere in which you can make rapid improvement with intensive training and hard work.

Golf and Your Health

There have been many assertions stated, and unfortunately many falsehoods made regarding the health effects of the sport of golf. The main health effect of golf lies in the fact that it is a leisurely sporting activity carried out in the fresh air. Just like walkers, the golfer is out in the fresh air for long periods of time and places only a fairly constant demand on his body.

Let us not place too great a measure on this - the demands on the body are not gigantic. It is only just as exhausting as a walk for several hours. The difference lies mainly in the amount of uphill stretches undertaken.

Nevertheless, it is our opinion that, in this day and age of an increase of the types of open-air leisure activities available, the sport of golf sits in somewhat of an oasis. An increase in the well-balanced inner feelings of the human being leads to better performance and more fun. In golf, the ambition to be able to strike the ball like the world class players one watches on television, does not normally lead to an overstraining of the body as one tries to copy them. Every golfer can try these shots out without any worry. It's fun to try and if it doesn't succeed there will hardly be any danger to one's health. Thus it cannot be emphasized enough, that the balanced sporting activity of golf has a positive effect on the human organism.

However, you should take good note that, if you do not prepare yourself well, your spine can suffer damage the better you play. This is because the pressure on the vertebra in the spine is at its greatest when the golfer reaches the return at the highest point of the swing, and at which point a lot of energy is being built up. This is why a lot of professional golf players have backbone problems.

Contrary to this, amateur golfers are more prone to injuries in the regions of the elbows and in the shoulder, knee and ankle joints. Generally

230

these are not too serious. Sometimes there can be problems in the carpal tunnels down which the tendons run in the fingers. This can be put down to using too hard a grip. Healthy nourishment (raw vegetables) works wonders and cannot be replaced by physiotherapy.

In other respects, the golf swing is a one-sided movement as distinct from Langlauf, swimming (crawl or backstroke) or jogging. In golf, one is continually pulling back on the one side and swinging through to the target on the other. Both sides of the body therefore develop differently.

Using the golf gymnastic exercises, which have been especially conceived for us by specialists, you can avoid and guard against any acute problems. The exercises take only a short time to do (5-10 minutes), and above all are carried out in a standing position. The problem of lying on wet grass, which in many places hampers exercising, is thus done away with. As we have said before in Part 1 (Golf Gymnastics), you will be able to do some additional good for your body if you can work together individually with a physiotherapist (or a graduate sports teacher).

What is healthy in golf:	This can be unhealthy:
• Fresh air	• The one-sided swing action
• Movement	• Pressure on the vertebra
• Walking for hours	• Draughts
• Regularity	• Potholes in the ground
	• Pressure of time
	• Pulling the golf trolley (one-sided pressure)

231

GOLF AND FITNESS

Fitness for golf combines several important functions. For one you have to be capable of concentrating. To be able to do this, you must work up to possess a certain degree of stamina. Good stamina goes hand-in-hand with the ability to resist tiredness. With this the endurance capability of your muscles will increase. In addition you will need strong stomach and back muscles which support your spine during the swing. In order to avoid and guard against injury, your muscles and joints must be warmed-up and made flexible. This is also important for the swing action, so that it is done in a relaxed and natural way.

STAMINA

You can build up your stamina if you spend a quarter of an hour, daily, either running, cycling or swimming intensely. It is important that you carry this out for at least 10-15 minutes at a time. You can also take a 40 minute run twice a week. If you can devote time to do all this for at least just over an hour in total, your body will reciprocate. How you split up your training doesn't matter, but the rule is: No shorter than ten minutes (preferably as long as 20 minutes), and at best 75 minutes total training per week.

232

GOLF GYMNASTICS

Starting Exercises

Diagram 113:

Stand upright - alternating - lift your right heel up behind your back and touch it with your left hand, then do the opposite using the left heel and right hand. Stretch both arms up as you change.

Diagram 114:
Still on the move - change over and do the same exercise but in front of the body.

Diagram 115:
Now change over and do it with the right elbow touching the left knee ...

235

Diagram 116:

... and so on, using the opposite elbow and knee.

Half-way

Diagram 117:

Pick up a golf-club. Hold it out horizontally in front of you just at the height of your belly-button (or choose any spot on the body!) and lift your knee up to touch the shaft.

237

Diagram 118:
Step over the club ...

238

Diagram 119:
... and carefully bring it up behind your body...

239

Diagram 120:
... and over your head until it is front of you again.

240

Diagram 121:
With the club in front of you again, continually change your hold from an underhand grip ...

241

Diagram 122:
... to an overhand grip.

Diagram 123:
Place the tips of your fingers on your shoulders and ...

243

Diagram 124:
... ensure your arms and shoulders form a straight line.

Diagram 125:
In this position turn your body from side to side ...

Diagram 126:
... and hold it for a few seconds each time - take care not to whip as you do!

246

Finishing Exercises

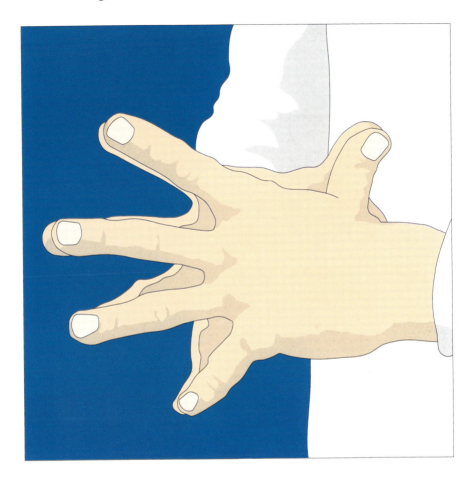

Diagram 127:
Press the tips of your fingers and thumbs together and push in and out to stretch the finger tendons.

247

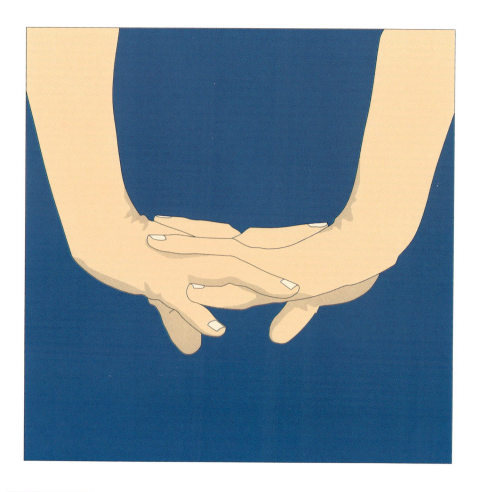

Diagram 128:

Join your hands together as shown and flex the hands and arms away from the body.

248

Diagram 129:

Finally, lay your hands on your diaphragm, shut your eyes and breathe normally (through your nose - not too deeply) so that your hands move up and down as they lay on your body. Do this for as long as it is still comfortable.

"Winding Down"

'Winding down' in golf has little to do with health - it is more to do with the opportunity to revise, and, with the experiences still fresh in the mind, work on the swings you have made in the last round. You will be able to correct any mistakes you were making as well as enlarge on the good points and any new experiences you have had. For the really ambitious golf sportsmen of you, it is well worth rounding off a day of golf with a psychological "cooling down" session. After either a particularly good or particularly bad tournament, it makes sense to put yourself 'on the mat' again. With the following training exercise you can achieve both:

Training Exercise

a) Do some shots with a medium iron.

b) Now hit some drives.

c) Carry out the shots which you liked doing the best during the round.

d) Use the feedback method - e.g. soak up the feeling as you stand in the follow through position for 20 seconds at the end of the stroke.

e) Continue hitting the ball - each time using a lower club until you round off the day with a short pitch.

A Few Simple Truths

THE CONCEPT OF MOVEMENT IN GOLF

The concept of movement is based on a single idea for the whole action. One talks of an 'idea in the mind's eye' or of a 'thought process' in connection with the swing. Certain parts of the movement serve sometimes to reflect a number of different 'ideas' or 'thoughts', but at the same time several technical details will always be run together. Therefore the 'idea' or 'thought process' is the medium with which we can particularly achieve improvement in our game. It is simpler to train with one idea in mind rather than with several all at the same time. Nevertheless the 'idea' or 'thought process' will contain all the information we need. The most important point about the various 'ideas' or 'thought processes' is that we perceive something from them.

Today one can measure how the muscles contract very slightly, even when one merely thinks of a particular movement or action. The assumption is that one knows the movement involved already. It is exactly this mechanism which one uses for 'mental training' - the muscles required to carry out the action and movement are the ones which will move. A good sense of the 'idea' or 'thought process' is always combined with genuine body reactions, assuming that we understand and know the movement and action in some form or other.

For the same action or part of the action in the golf swing, there are numerous various 'ideas' and 'thought processes' which can exist in the mind. The art, which is up to the coach and the player also himself, is to discover which of the 'ideas' and 'thought processes' he can react to.

THE SWEETSPOT IS SMALL

There is hardly another kind of sport in which the number of factors, at the same time as having an influence on one's performance, is so large, and in which the equipment (the golf-club, ball etc.,) itself does not allow

251

any room for the player to make a mistake. The golf-club is roughly 45 inches long and the clubhead minutely small - when, for example, compared to the tennis racquet. The 'sweetspot' - the point which transfers the optimum energy - is even smaller. This spot - from which the ball receives its optimal trajectory - is about the size of a finger nail. Using the same construction methods as we have seen in tennis (enlarged racquet heads, use of graphite and similar other materials), golf-club manufacturers have tried to enlarge the sweetspot. By doing so, some of the feeling (feedback) is lost - one of the reasons why so many world class players still use steel shafts.

If you try to concentrate on hitting the ball exactly on the sweetspot every time, then golf will be practically impossible unless you are playing it continually all the time - for example as a professional player does.

Once you can accept this fact, you will find it easier to take the necessary individual steps, despite this, to improve your game.

Everyone, who has had anything to do with golf, will know that the game requires patience, humility, restraint, self-discipline, conscientiousness, honesty, modesty and not least passion.

It is often the perfectionists amongst golf players who become particularly disappointed and dejected. When one often attaches perfectionism to the top players, it is still the ability to improvise and to recognize one's own limitations which has been more important on the road to success. Even the best players in the world have always emphasized, that there were only a handful of shots, if any at all, in the round which were that good to be called perfect.

So it is worthwhile having a little more forbearance and understanding for your own inadequacies.

"FEEL OF THE BALL" AND GOLF

The expression 'feel of the ball' is very difficult to imagine. Scientists argue and have very differing opinions, even today, as to how much of this mystic ability the human being is born with, and how much can be learnt.

One distinct advantage in golf is that the ball is stationary - unlike tennis where it is moving at variously changing and rapid speed. At the same time, the particular fact that only if you do everything correctly a perfect impact will be made, leads on to produce fears that prevent one from doing so in the first place.

When putting, these fears can create uncontrollable reflexes (called "yips") in the muscles of the lower arms just at the moment of impact - even pros experience these.

Experience has shown that even people, with little 'feel for the ball', can still be capable of reaching enormous performance levels in golf. Such people are those who are unable to develop their coordination of move-ment in the types of sport where the ball is on the move. Since the golf swing is somewhat stereotyped, this allows a relatively high degree of attainment to be achieved by constant practice. In certain varied circumstances, as far as it goes regarding the 'feel for the ball', the more talented golfer will rise above those who are less so endowed.

ETIQUETTE - AS PER THE 'PENALTY SPOT'

In some parts of the world the sport of golf has unfortunately not yet unshackled itself from social prejudices. In some golf-clubs other things come often into play rather than the sport itself. In a number of tournaments such as amateur team championships, every now and again one hears of unsportsmanlike behaviour. The name of professional golf is, on the other hand, well renown for its unique, world-wide maintenance of 'fair play' in all its aspects. Ever since golf was first played, it has been customary that

Diagram 130:
It is all a matter of your attitude whether you are easily distracted by what is happening around you.

254

players stay quiet and still while a shot is being played. We all learned this habit when we started ourselves. For Paul Gascoigne it is different.

He learned that etiquette played no part when he had to convert a penalty shot. Sometimes hundreds of thousands of people were screaming and yelling as he concentrated himself on taking the shot.

It is a question of adaptability whether you are disturbed if someone talks while you are playing the ball (see Diagram 130). If you decide that from today, you will not start afresh to take your shot, or react in some other way if there are disturbances, it will only be a question of a few weeks until you have the equanimity to go ahead, like Paul Gascoigne shooting a penalty in front of 120,000 fans. You will have of course already spotted that it is a question of your attitude rather than your concentration. We recommend that from now on you do not bother about picking up any more etiquette. You can decide this for yourself, and you need not go around acclaiming this from the roof-tops! *On the other hand you should, of course as before, stand still when someone else is playing a shot.*

GOOD GOLF IS 'BORING'?

You will realize that successful golf is not particularly spectacular. The long-time professionals almost always land on the fairway and the green first time. Only when the fairways are narrow does it get a little exciting - at least for the player. He will choose a club with which he will be sure to land on the fairway. Only in situations in which, by using a lower number club there would hardly be any safe advantage ensuing, will he decide to risk a drive. That is why, at some holes, you will see the pros with a 1-iron instead of a driver.

If you watch a professional tournament, you will ascertain that even the particularly good rounds are not very spectacular. Of course there are exceptions. Alexander Ceijka probably plays in a more exciting manner than Bernhard Langer. Ballesteros plays clearly more appealingly than

255

Montgomerie. A round of 6 under PAR is often a round without hitting the green or without an eagle, but with many standard shots onto the middle of the fairway and green.

The secret lies in the art of choosing the moment to take a calculated risk. There are many golf-courses which have holes having both a conservative approach to the flag as well a tricky route. Mostly the tricky route is so dangerous that even the pro will not attempt it. If he was to come unstuck, only once, during a four-round tournament, to gain two shots on another day would not help him as they would balance out. Choosing the safe route he always gives himself the chance, with a good approach shot, to go out with a birdie as well.

Carry on playing 'boringly'! It will be personally more exciting for you and you will have more fun because you will play more successfully.

In our opinion one sees too few amateurs who select the route forward strategically enough to match their own playing capabilities. Be more often prepared to choose a club, with which you will only reach perhaps 150 yards, but will land, for all, that on the fairway safely in front of a hazard and not in it!

Make sure you can react to all the varying situations you will meet on the golf-course. Without delaying too long, answer all the challenges correctly. In „Straight Golf", you will have discovered an answer for most of the situations on the golf-course - whether it is a high-lipped bunker shot, a shot out of the rough with a water hazard in front of the green, or whether it is a player who is chatting all the time just as you are trying to drop your chip dead.

Work up your pre-shot routine and play the ball - unspectacularly but successfully.

Examples of Golf-Club Sets

Clubs for the first experience of golf
7-iron
Putter

**Beginner's set of clubs
(the first months)**
3-Wood
5-iron
7-iron
9-iron
Putter
(all clubs are R-shafted (see note1))

**Advanced Beginner's set of clubs
(first year)**
3-Wood
7-Wood
3-iron
5-iron
7-iron
9-iron
Chipper
Sandwedge
Putter
(all clubs are R-shafted)

Set of clubs for Handicap 28 (UK)/30 (Europe) (has played for several years-infrequently)
3-Wood
5-Wood
7-Wood

9-Wood
4-iron
5-iron
6-iron
7-iron
8-iron
9-iron
PW
SW
Chipper
Putter
(all clubs are R-shafted)

**Set of clubs for Handicap 20
(plays infrequently)**
1-Wood
4-Wood
7-Wood
9-Wood
4-iron
5-iron
6-iron
7-iron
8-iron
9-iron
PW
SW
Chipper
Putter
(all clubs are R-shafted)

**Set of clubs for Handicap 18
(plays regulary)**
1-Wood
3-Wood
5-Wood
7-Wood

257

3-iron
4-iron
5-iron
6-iron
7-iron
8-iron
9-iron
PW
SW
Putter
(all clubs are R-shafted)

Set of clubs for Handicap 6

1-Wood
3-Wood
5-Wood
3-iron
4-iron
5-iron
6-iron
7-iron
8-iron
9-iron
PW
SW
Lofter
Putter
(Woods - S-shafted; Irons - as required R or S-shafted (see Note 1))

Club Set Selection and Equipment - Rainer Mund

1-Wood	9 Degrees King Cobra Deep Face (Strong)
3-Wood	15 Degrees Metalwood Taylor Made S400U
1-iron	Ping BC (Red dot)

3-iron	S400U	Cobra
4-iron	S400U	Cobra
5-iron	S400U	Cobra
6-iron	S400U	Cobra
7-iron	S400U	Cobra
8-iron	S400U	Cobra
9-iron	S400U	Cobra
PW	R400U	Yonex 49 Degrees
SW	R400U	Yonex 55 Degrees
Lofter		Cobra 61 Degrees
Putter		Ping Anser

Shoes:	Adidas
Ball:	Titleist Tour 100 Balata
Gloves:	Foot-Foy

Note 1:	'R' = Regular
	'S' = Stiff

English Titles
Meyer & Meyer Publishing